Web Diva Wisdom

How to Find, Hire, and Partner with the Right Web Designer for You

LISA B STAMBAUGH

ISBN: 1493756451
ISBN-13: 9781493756452
Library of Congress Control Number: 2014906546
CreateSpace Independent Publishing Platform
North Charleston, South Carolina

I'm surrendering myself to the realities of the Internet.

—*Scott Adams*

Sometimes you have to be a diva. If you are strong, if you have vision, if you are an artist, you have to do what you believe in. And if you get called a diva for it, then so what?

—*Jessie J.*

To Carol,
Build a kickass website
and rule the web!

— Lisa
The web diva

Contents

Introduction

How can I prepare myself to get the very most from my relationship with my web designer, and how can I make it the most productive and successful partnership possible?

In the Internet world, change happens quickly. Styles evolve. Tools improve. Technologies advance. Audiences grow and learn. However, common sense approaches have not changed much over time, including the basics of business skills, logic, organization, process-based thinking, mutual trust, and respectful behavior.

This book is designed to share the tips and tricks that will:

- enable you to choose the right web designer for you

- allow your web designer to work more efficiently on your behalf

- help you collaborate to develop the best website for your services and products

As a freelance web designer with fifteen-plus years of experience developing over five hundred websites for individuals, small-to-medium-sized businesses, and nonprofit organizations, I've developed processes, checklists, and templates to get the job done. No stone has been left unturned in uncovering every little detail of the website design process: the best ways to approach the many tasks and challenges, the common mistakes that clients make, and the things they do that can drive a web designer crazy!

This book is a compilation of this information in a format that will be useful to anyone working with a professional web designer. In the end, you will:

- control the project cost and schedule

- reduce errors

- avoid rework

- minimize your frustration

- shorten the timeline to launch your website

- create the best possible website to meet your goals in terms of budget, timeline, and functionality

The material is organized in standalone sections. You can read the entire book now and get value from it, but it can also be relevant as a step-by-step resource, to be read in sections, based on where you are in the process. Reading this book will give you the tools to get the most out of a working relationship with your web designer so you can create the best website possible for your needs.

Everything you need to know about working with a web designer, in the order you need to know it.

This book should be an essential reference for anyone working with—or planning to hire—a web designer. Its goals are to provide basic guidance for the newcomer embarking on the process for the first time, as well as to offer lessons and process improvements for those already working with a web designer.

Whether you are ready to partner with a web designer for a new website, a redesign project, or major updates to an existing website, you'll find helpful guidelines, tips, and best practices.

As a client, you are ultimately the creator and owner of your website. If you don't collaborate with your web designer and actively participate in the process, you won't end up with the website of your dreams.

Hiring someone to design your website should not be a one-time, short-term project but rather the start of a long—and hopefully productive and successful—business partnership. Let this book be your guide to getting the most out of your relationship with your current or future web designer.

How This Book Is Organized

Part 1: Building Blocks

Understand where you are in the website lifecycle. Know the basic building blocks of any website, including the players.

Part 2: Do Your Homework

Pinpoint budget and timeline constraints. Do your prework by gathering information, conducting competitive analysis, identifying your audience, and drafting a marketing plan.

Part 3: Discovery

Search for qualified candidate web designers that fit your requirements. Initiate contact, complete the investigation and proposal process, and check references.

Part 4: Development

Hire your web designer and build a working relationship of open and honest communication, trust, respect, delegation, and partnership. Design and build your website, understand the creative process, and actively participate in iterative development and refinement.

Part 5: Delivery

Launch and announce your website. Keep your website current in both content and presentation. Know the options if your web designer relationship status changes.

The Plan of Attack

If your organization currently has a website or intends to develop one in the near future, you should fit into one of these five scenarios.

A. You do not have a website but know that you need one.

- Read Parts 1, 2, 3, 4, and 5.

B. You have a website that meets your current needs, and you are working with a web designer that you want to keep.

- Read Parts 4 and 5.

C. You have a website that meets your current needs, and you need to find a new web designer.

- Read parts 3, 4, and 5.

D. You have a website that needs replacing, and you are working with a web designer that you want to keep.

- Read Parts 2, 4, and 5.

E. You have a website that needs replacing, and you need to find a new web designer.

- Read Parts 2, 3, 4, and 5.

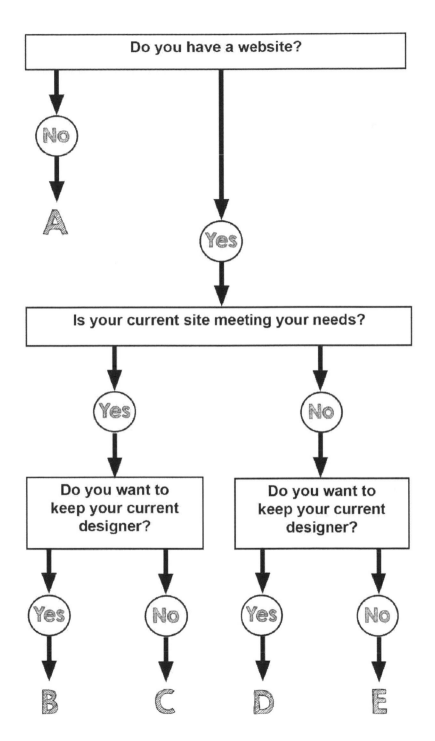

Vocabulary

In order to make this as readable as possible—and still be applicable to the majority of readers—I've made some assumptions about how I represent both web designers and the people that hire them.

For example, I've used the term *organization* to refer to any business, company, nonprofit organization, or individual that might be hiring someone to design their website.

Similarly, I've assumed that all organizations have at least two people involved, whether owners, employees, contractors, or partners. So in exercises where I'm counting on the reader to take the lead, I've used the terms *we* and *our*. In your case, it might really be *I* and *my*, but everything should still make sense.

When it comes to web designers, I've also generalized this term to include anyone you might hire to do any part of the design, development, implementation, or programming of your website. In Part 1, I cover some details about the various people or organizations you might hire. In the end, whether you hire an individual, several independent individuals, or a company, the same advice will apply.

When I talk about the people or organizations that have hired me, I always refer to them as clients. I choose to make a distinction between *customers* (those who purchase in a single transaction and have no long-term relationship with the vendor, such as someone buying a latte at the local coffee shop) and *clients* (those who maintain a consistent working relationship in partnership over a longer time frame). Your own organization might have either clients or customers, or a combination of both—but in this book, I'm going to refer to them as clients.

PART 1
Building Blocks

Understand where you are in the website lifecycle. Know the basic building blocks of any website, including the players.

What do you wish you had known before working with a web designer?

"I had already once created my own website. It takes real money to hire a web designer, and that's what always stopped me from hiring one. Once I finally did, I wished I had known before how much cleaner the website [would] look; [how my business has a] more professional appearance…because of it; and how easy it is to change stuff on it."

"I was not prepared for all that was required to tell a company's story via website. Ideally, I would have been ready with decisions, rather than struggle to wrap myself around the process."

"You need to invest lots of your own time to clearly understand what you want before fully engaging a web designer. A web designer can help coach you through the process, but you need to figure out what you want and how to convey it."

"Gather the information ahead of time…Arm your designer with the tools to get the job done quickly and efficiently."

"How important the chemistry is between you and the designer! Many people have website design skills, but it's even more key to understand how you will work together."

"The questions to ask to select a website designer that would match my vision, message, and clients, and if they were actually competent to complete the job."

—Survey responses

You may think it's about the tools, but web design is first and foremost a *process*

The tools used to implement the website are not as important as you think they are; the tools are not what define the messaging or behavior of the website. You can use any number of different languages—or even different approaches using the same language—and arrive at the same end result. Website visitors have no idea how it was programmed, unless they know how to look at the source code. When you talk to a web designer, your best bet is to explain what you want to see on the website, not how to implement it. Let the implementation decisions rest with the person who will be handling that work.

When it comes down to it, web design is a process. Long before the process involves graphic design, writing of text, and programming, it involves business analysis, thoughtful consideration of the hoped-for visitor audience, and an evaluation of purposes, objectives, and measurable results.

Effective web design extends far beyond integrating words and pictures into a visible page

You say you want to design and implement your own website. That's great. The tools are available, and you can enjoy learning some basics of programming and development. You can maintain complete artistic control and derive satisfaction from seeing your ideas come to life on the screen. If you have the time to spend on ramping up your skills, so much the better.

However, there is much more to web design than merely having the time to play around on your computer. When you hire a professional web designer, you are not just paying for time; you are paying for knowledge. You are paying for training and for experience that only comes from a combination of being on the job and attending the school of hard knocks. You pay today for what the web designer knows today, but he or she continues to learn, so in the future you pay for what he or

3

she will have learned. You're paying for someone to do some design and programming work. You're also paying for his or her education, experience, computers, software, training, insurance, marketing, phone, other bills, and the time to answer your questions, phone calls, and e-mail messages. Come to think of it, those are the same expenses that your clients cover when they hire you for whatever services you provide.

Of course, an appealing and aesthetically pleasing website is your goal. However, your website must also appear intuitive, be highly functional, communicate unambiguously, and connect with the targeted audience. Ease of use, cross-browser compatibility, and cross-device functionality are also key factors in producing a successful website.

Pay for the skills of a trained and experienced web professional, and free yourself to be an expert in your own field

You are proficient in your area of expertise, and clients come to you because they trust a professional to get the job done correctly and efficiently. Consider the same perspective for your web designer. Find and hire a qualified professional, and trust that person to get the job done for you in a timely and effective way, following current standards.

You are (or should be) an expert in your specialty but are probably not an expert in what it takes to create an exceptional website.

An experienced web designer must have skills encompassing programming, graphic design, writing, business understanding, client focus, customer service, and problem solving.

In other words, an experienced web designer must be able to:

- program in several languages using standard applications and environments

4

- evaluate technical approaches and make choices

- recognize the constant change and trends of technology, standards, usability, and design—including programming techniques, viewing devices, search engine optimization, and social media

- create original artwork using standard applications and software

- understand graphic design theory

- modify or edit graphic assets created or provided by others

- create original written content based on client input and draft materials

- edit content provided by clients

- clearly articulate information to a wide audience

- organize and position materials to accurately represent the client's product or service offering

- understand basic business principles and the activities involved with client interaction

- manage budget, schedule, and feature set requirements

- triage and prioritize input from multiple sources and resolve conflicts

- interact with a variety of people in a cross section of industries and businesses, spanning a wide range of ages, experience, and levels of technical understanding

- patiently answer questions in a nontechnical way appropriately suited to the client's level of understanding

- replicate, debug, and resolve bugs and problems

Do it yourself and save money—at the expense of results, functionality, and productivity

Positive:

- There is no delay in getting started.

- You have complete control over the schedule.

- There is no one to contradict your decisions.

- You have an initial lower cost for labor.

- There are free tools that might also include free integrated hosting.

Negative:

- Your website has a less professional implementation and presentation.

- There are many unknowns: you won't even know what you don't know.

- You need to find someone to delegate to if you are unable to do (or complete) the work.

- You are already busy running your business, which has to be your top priority.

- You have an initial higher cost for software and time to learn.

- You run the risk of encountering technical issues you are unable to resolve.

- You run the risk of spending more money on other items, due to your lack of knowledge and experience.

Hire a web designer for a more professional result, but expect to spend more

Positive:

- Your website has a more professional implementation and presentation, including improved usability and maintainability.

- You get exactly what you want by explaining it to someone who knows how to do it.

- Your website is not a cookie-cutter result, looking like many other websites.

- You have an expert resource available to help answer questions and solve problems.

- A pro is dedicated and committed to your project and can focus on it, while you focus on what you do best: running your business.

- You get better return on the time and money invested (ROI)—where return is measured by increased traffic, sales, and client engagement.

- You have a shorter elapsed time to the end result.

- There is no cost or learning curve time for software.

Negative:

- You have a higher initial cost for labor.

- You have to deal with the emotionally challenging situation of putting your trust in someone else to do what you want.

- There could be a possible delay of the project until your preferred web designer is available.

- There may be unpredictable issues if the web designer is difficult to work with (and this is not discovered until you are into the process).

Exercise: Do we have the technical skills?

Our organization (or someone in our organization):

- ☐ has relevant programming experience
- ☐ has access to the necessary software applications and tools
- ☐ is willing to buy the necessary tools and software applications
- ☐ knows how to use these applications and tools
- ☐ is willing to learn how to use these applications and tools
- ☐ knows how to convert photos and illustrations into an optimal website format
- ☐ has graphic design experience
- ☐ understands how search engines will be used by our target audience
- ☐ knows how to market an organization, as well as its products and services, through a website
- ☐ knows the difference between writing for websites and print collateral (such as brochures or flyers)
- ☐ understands the mechanics of domain registration and hosting
- ☐ is willing to manage ongoing upgrades to the website and development software, based on trends and Internet use evolution

Exercise: Do we have the Internet knowledge and logistics skills?

Our organization (or someone in our organization):

☐ has access to a PC, Mac, smartphone, and tablet for testing across platforms (or equivalent testing tools)

☐ knows the standards in use today for monitor size and display resolution, including mobile devices

☐ understands how the various browsers and devices interpret the programming to display a website

☐ knows how to collect website traffic and visitor statistics

☐ knows how to analyze and use this data to make changes that improve the website

☐ is willing to learn what we don't know

☐ has the time to learn what we don't know

☐ has the time to make maintenance changes to our website on an ongoing basis

Web Designers and Developers

The terms *web designer* and *web developer* are often used interchangeably, but they are not necessarily the same

Web design is the visible, customer-facing part of the website. A web designer focuses on what your website looks like and how visitors will interact with it. Good web designers use proven professional design principles to create a great-looking website. They also understand usability requirements and know how to create a website that customers can easily navigate and use to find the information they need.

Web development is the back-end implementation of the website, the programming, and interactions on the pages. A web developer focuses on how your website works and the tasks that visitors need to accomplish. Professional web developers have expertise in a number of programming languages and approaches. They know how to determine which implementation methods are best for your project and needs and the keys to keeping a website running effectively and efficiently. They understand how to structure the website so that changes can be integrated later without compromising functionality and performance. They know how to implement back-end capabilities such as slideshows, forms, and online payment.

For many smaller organizations, it makes sense to find one resource to handle both design and development

Some designers know a fair amount about programming. And many programmers understand the principles of design and usability. Some amount of overlap is critical to getting the best possible result from those in either profession. In your search, if you want to work with only one person, you need to ask the right questions and know what candidates are capable of providing.

Many organizations can't (or don't want to) hire both a web designer and a web developer to get the job done. They want one resource who

10

will take them through the entire process, start to finish. Dealing with two phases, plus the handoff between two contractors, is more than many organizations are willing to handle.

If you hire two different resources (people or organizations) to get both jobs done, you need to understand the difference between their responsibilities and orchestrate the handoff and communication process—and that may be more overhead than is necessary.

When it comes to hiring a single resource, it might be one person or one business that includes multiple employees to handle the different parts of the process. What I do *not* recommend is hiring one person to do the design work and then handing that finished design to a completely independent resource who was not part of the design process. You want a single resource, and if there will be communication or handoff issues, at least a company will have that built into their internal process so you don't have to deal with it.

The rest of this book relies heavily on the assumption that your organization will find and work with a single resource, to be referred to as "web designer."

Determine whether you will best be served by working with a company or an individual

Web designers range from rookies to experienced large companies or agencies. Any one of them may be right for you, but it will help to know the options before you start looking.

You can find web design companies in any metropolitan area or larger city. On the positive side, they have a team to support your project, so it's unlikely to stall out, partially finished. On the other hand, you may not have a one-on-one relationship with a single person responsible for your project. Companies will typically charge more than freelancers, as they usually have larger overhead expenses, possibly including office space. As a plus, since a company is depending on a team of people to provide all necessary skills, it's not necessary to have one person who can "do it all."

If you're reading this book, you may not be a candidate for working with *large* companies, as they are typically more expensive than small companies or freelancers and usually take on larger projects. Then again, if you have the resources and are considered a large enough project for them, it could be the right solution. A larger company will have more overhead expenses that drive up its cost, but it is also typically more established and has made more of a commitment to stay in business.

Freelancers come in all flavors, from newcomers to the very experienced. Experienced freelancers may have worked for one or more companies and eventually decided to start their own businesses. Or it could be that they never worked for another web design company, but they've been on their own for a long time so are experienced. Experienced freelancers usually have the skills and tools at hand to do a good, complete, reliable job, at a reasonable cost.

One challenge is confirming that the solo freelancer has the required skills and business stability to meet *your* needs. If you find a qualified, reliable freelancer, you will be able to work with that person to build the website you need and deserve.

The risk is in confirming the actual experience level of a freelancer, as well as the related skills—both technical and interpersonal. Just because his or her website says the designer is good, it doesn't mean that's the case. With a freelancer, you'll need to do extra homework to check references and confirm the viability of his or her business.

When working with an inexperienced web designer, supervise vigilantly, and demand course correction immediately

If you select a web designer with limited experience, you will probably end up with a website, but it may not be as professional as you would like. It may not happen on schedule or at the estimated cost, and it may not be optimally produced to survive through the next few years. Given your budget constraints, this might be a reasonable trade-off—as long as you are aware of the issues.

Let's be realistic: everyone starts somewhere in this business. In the best possible scenario, the new web designer actually brings experience from another job or has implemented a number of websites as a volunteer or for personal projects.

If someone is new to freelance web design but has a long employment record in related work, he or she could (and should) be low-risk. That's my story: I was working in software engineering, information technology, and web design at larger high-tech companies before setting out on my own. So I had the training and experience of the actual work to be done, just not the experience of running my own business. On my own, I was building and maintaining websites as a volunteer for my children's schools, for a number of local nonprofit organizations, and a few local businesses—all to build experience and establish a portfolio of reliable references. Some of those initial websites from the mid-1990s are still my responsibility, although they have all been redesigned several times to keep up with changing standards and client needs.

If you're planning to hire an inexperienced web designer, you must evaluate this person's ability and potential to provide an end product that meets your requirements. You may need to put in extra time to supervise, provide immediate feedback, and do more homework on your own. You should have a well-defined list of intermediate deliverables. At the first sign of problems, either stop the project to find another resource or take the time to make major course corrections.

Don't hire a family member—unless he or she is, in fact, a web designer

I know, that sounds harsh. But I've had many people come to me and say, "My brother volunteered to make a website for me," or, "My daughter in high school said she could make a website for me, because she'd like to learn how to do it." And then, guess what? It didn't quite go as planned.

If a relative is an option, try this little exercise: pretend this person is not your relative. Would you still hire him or her? If you're not sure, just run through the process outlined later in this book. If your relative really can jump though the hoops, then you can think about hiring him or her. In my experience, none of the casual "it sounds like fun and I want to learn how to do this" folks would pass the tests I have put forth.

Realistically, there is a good exception to this rule: if your family member is actually a professional web designer, it's got a much better chance of working out. Even so, that's not always the case.

One of my long-term clients has a brother who is a professional web designer with a long track record of accomplishments at larger high-tech companies. He designed her original website, but when he was constrained by demands from his "real" job, her website update requests were always put on the back burner. In fact, I knew her brother and had even worked with him back in my corporate days. He's an experienced and talented web designer—but when push comes to shove, his employer is going to pull rank on his baby sister. So eventually it made more business sense for her to pay me to get the job done. Free services from her brother were of little use if he did not have the bandwidth to provide them.

No single web designer is a specialist in all aspects of design and development

The Internet is too far-reaching now for any one person to be a specialist in *all* aspects of it. Don't assume that all web designers excel at everything from search engine optimization to usability, from graphic design to programming. Good web designers focus on the areas they are willing to work in, maintaining current education and training and learning more about those areas. The pragmatic ones will clearly state whether or not a specific implementation or feature is within their domain of expertise.

While there is a basic set of skills and knowledge that all web designers should have, some specialties require extra training, aptitude, and experience—not to mention the additional time to stay abreast of the latest innovations in each area.

No web designer should tell you that he or she is an expert at *all* of it. It's just not possible to know that much, especially at the rate the technology changes and improves. Savvy web designers will take on projects that depend most on the skills and expertise they *do* possess, as they are more likely to have a good outcome. If a project comes their way and is not a good fit, they will decline and possibly help you find someone who is a better fit. As is true with any career, unless the person has the skills, desire, and passion to do his or her best work, he or she may not do a great job for you and could eventually resent taking on the project.

Web design and print design require different skills

Some web designers provide print design services, and some print designers design websites. This makes sense as there is an overlap in the technical tools and software that are used for both types of projects and some similarity in the design principles in use.

An experienced graphic designer does not necessarily excel at both web and print work. The mechanical processes are different between the media. A web designer must understand programming, usability, browsers, and typical behaviors of online readers. A print designer must understand the printing process, different hardcopy presentation formats, and the way readers make use of print collateral.

You may very well find a designer capable of providing both services. If you plan to hire a print designer who claims website design experience, confirm the actual results by visiting the websites that he or she has designed.

I had one terrible experience where a client came to me with a design produced by a print designer. When I printed the design on paper and looked at it, in fact it was quite attractive. On the other hand, programming it was a nightmare, and in the end, the navigation was completely unworkable, between the location and the presentation. I tried suggesting some changes to my client, in the hopes of salvaging the design. In the end, we could not make it work as designed. Through

major revisions and compromises, we came up with a workable website,
but it was not without angst on both sides. That project was the one that
made me establish a policy of not taking on implementation projects
where someone else did the design work unless I was also involved with
the design to provide feedback.

Web designers only *seem* to be online 24-7

Many web designers rely on e-mail, web, and social media interaction for just about all of the input around their work. They may check and respond to e-mail frequently—but that does not mean they are available to work all the time.

You may be misled into thinking that web designers are available to handle your requests at night, on weekends, or on holidays. You send e-mail on Saturday because you are working on Saturday, so you assume that your web designer must be working on Saturday as well. It's fine to send requests at night or on the weekend, just don't assume you'll get a response until the next working day. If you do send a request during nonbusiness hours, and it can wait until the next business day, be sure to say so in your message.

Personally, I find it difficult to *not* check e-mail frequently. That doesn't mean I'm always working, but I try to be available for emergencies or questions—even when on vacation (I know, that's my problem, not the client's). Sometimes, a simple response saying "Got your message, will do it tomorrow" is all a client really needs in order to know that his or her request is now in the queue and will get my attention when it's his or her turn. It only takes a minute to answer the message, even if the work is not going to be done immediately.

Web design is not generally a nine-to-five office job

The career of website design is about hard work in a very public forum, dealing with difficult decisions, committing to excellence, and understanding ever-changing technology. It means being on call 24-7, dealing with emergencies, and a willingness to do some work that is unbillable. It means interacting with many independent clients, each of whom may be demanding attention on any day, at any time.

Along with the planned and predictable work, an urgent or time-critical request may come in unexpectedly. I describe my own day as that of a triage nurse in the ER—I constantly have to juggle incoming requests with the items already on my to-do list. A website that is not breathing needs more immediate attention than one with a broken finger.

There is always the necessity of doing some unbillable work in the interest of a successful outcome. And who doesn't expect to put in some time answering e-mail or phone calls or discussing potential projects? Of course not every minute of effort is billable. On the other hand, clients tend to assume that the web designer's time is unlimited and available—and generously contributed to the project.

Identify a reliable tech support resource other than your web designer

Even though they are tech savvy, web designers are not your personal free tech support department for all problems or challenges related to your own computing environment.

This includes items such as:

- purchasing, setting up, debugging, and fixing computers
- purchasing, setting up, debugging, and fixing other devices, including phones, printers, modems, routers, and tablets
- installing, configuring, debugging, or training on the use of software

The key word here is *free*. It doesn't mean you should not ask, but you should assume that this is billable work. Don't call your web designer for help with computers and hardware, unless you already have an agreement that this is within the scope of the project for which he or she is being hired.

Website Mechanical Components

In a nutshell, for any website you need to do the following:

1. Search for an available domain name.

2. Register your chosen domain name.

3. Set up a website hosting package.

Once these three steps are completed, anyone can design and create your website, as long as he or she has access to the accounts.

Domain name registration is somewhat like registering a unique, custom license plate for your website. There can only be a single owner of any domain name at any time. Once you own a domain name (and continue to pay the bills), you can be assured that you are the only one able to use that domain name. You can move your domain to another registrar at any time. So in the event that you made a less-than-optimal choice the first time, you can always move to a new registrar later, at minimal expense.

If domain registration is the equivalent of registering your unique, custom website license plate with the DMV-equivalent of the Internet, hosting is somewhat like buying a parking space in a public garage. While the original files to create your website reside on an individual computer (presumably that of your web designer), the website is not visible to the public unless those files are uploaded to a server that is accessible to the Internet. That's where hosting comes in—it's that public parking space that the world can see when they drive by.

The Internet Corporation for Assigned Names and Numbers (ICANN) is a nonprofit corporation that was created in 1998 to take on the responsibility of assigning unique identifiers (the letters and numbers used to form a domain name) across the world.

Register your domain with a reputable and accredited registrar

The existence of ICANN means that you and I—and everyone else looking for a domain name—have plenty of choices when it comes to looking for a place to register domain names. There are many different domain name registrars and domain name resellers. It is important that you chose a domain name registrar that is ICANN-accredited or choose a reseller that is affiliated with an ICANN-accredited domain registrar.

In most cases, domain registration is something you set up once and then rarely have to deal with—unless you want to make a change in your service provider. Where you register your domain will not impact the performance of your website. In the event that you need help with managing it, or have to communicate with tech support, some registrars are easier to deal with than others. But in the end, where you register your domain name has no physical impact on the website.

There is no requirement to have domain registration and website hosting with the same service provider. The tools are in place to mechanically link your domain name and hosting, no matter where either element was purchased. However, if you have a choice, one benefit of using the same provider for both is that you only deal with one service provider when it comes to support, billing, and administration.

Don't select your domain registrar based on price

No matter how attractive it may be, don't select a registrar based simply on price. They won't all charge the same amount, but the difference is small, compared to the cost of the website project. Time spent on the phone with technical support can far outweigh any cost savings.

Just recently, a client had a billing issue to resolve with her registrar. She spent over five hours on the phone, between on-hold time and conversations. In the end, her issue was resolved, but she'd invested plenty of time and frustration. And I'm not even including my (nonbillable) time to answer questions and send follow-up e-mail information about alternate solutions!

A lesson here is to go with a reputable, large-name service provider with a good reputation for customer support and responsiveness. Reviews and opinions are available on discussion boards and forums. Simply use a search engine to find commentary about service providers of any kind, starting with a string such as "*name* customer service review" (replace *name* with the name of the company you are investigating).

It can be difficult to change domain name ownership, once it's been established

Would you let someone else register the personalized license plate for your car? Would you let someone else put his or her name on the deed to your house? Would you let a relative stranger be a cosigner on your bank account? Don't let someone else own your domain name. Your friend, child, neighbor, or web designer may say they are doing you a favor by setting up the domain name. But what happens if they are no longer around to help you? Will they pay the renewal bills?

If it were easy to change ownership without a series of checks and balances, people would hijack domain names all the time. The process to resolve domain ownership disputes can involve faxing identifying information (drivers' licenses, business licenses) for both the current and new owners. If the current domain owner is not interested in participating or can't be located, it can be very difficult and time-consuming to reclaim the domain name until such time as it expires—assuming the other person doesn't renew it.

In one of those "why didn't you ask me first" situations, my cousin came to me with a disturbing story: the person hired to create her website had also registered the domain name in his ownership. Then he left the web business and was no longer interested in being responsible for her domain renewal fees. Needless to say, this caused her no end of grief, trying to track him down and get the registration renewal bills paid.

Once I was enlisted to untangle this mess, we spent several months going through the registrar's formal dispute resolution process. This involved faxing of a number of identifying items, writing up a detailed explanation of her business, and showing how her name was associated with the business. It was my cousin's good fortune to have a very unusual name and to have used her own name for the domain as well. So it was difficult—but not impossible—to establish that the website and the business it represented were in fact about her.

Select a well-known hosting company with a stellar reputation for technical support

Low price should no longer be an influential factor in choosing hosting. While you may assume that pricing is a key decision-making factor, other issues may ultimately be more important, such as availability of technical support, functionality, and so on. Most of the hosting packages today provide ample storage space and bandwidth, plus many (or even unlimited) e-mail accounts.

Many of the big-name, national hosting providers have excellent backup systems, 24-7 technical support, and complete functionality. Even if you will not be the person dealing with them most of the time, this will make the process easier and more efficient for your web designer.

Keep an eye on the ever-shrinking cost of hosting

If you already have a website on a hosting package purchased several years ago, it would be smart to check whether a lower-cost alternative is available at your same hosting service provider. As recently as a few years ago, smaller hosting companies were charging much higher prices, and if clients don't think to ask about lower rates, they are still paying the higher ones.

In 2013, a client came to me with an original website first established in 1999. At that time they signed up for a hosting package that ran over $45 per month and were still paying it—even though comparable hosting has been available for $5 per month for many years. Their original web designer did not even suggest to them that a less expensive alternative might be available. Our first project before designing the new website was moving to new hosting. At a savings of $40 a month, that's $480 a year—not insignificant when compared to the cost of the new website!

You can defer purchase of the hosting package until after hiring a web designer

Unlike domain names, hosting packages are not unique. It's understandable that you may want to acquire a domain name as soon as you decide on it, to avoid letting someone else acquire it. However, hosting is not like that.

A hosting package is merely a parking spot for your website, and once you own the domain name, you don't need hosting to protect it. If you don't have hosting at the time you decide to look for a web designer, you should wait until you hire that person and take his or her recommendations. He or she will know the best package and pricing for your needs. He or she may also have discounts available at certain vendors or may recommend some vendors over others, based on features, usability, and tech support.

Many designers have affiliate associations with their favorite hosting companies. This can save you money and maybe even give them a small commission as a result of your purchase. Another advantage of using a hosting company based on your web designer's recommendation: your web designer will be familiar with their back-end systems and control panel, so he or she can work more efficiently.

It happens all too frequently that clients come to me with hosting at companies with terrible tech support, limited capabilities, or a bad reputation for follow-through with issues. In that case, it's often worth the effort for me to help them move to new hosting. This may not even be billable work for me, but spending an hour to move to a system that will improve my own productivity (and avoid aggravation) is well worth it.

Don't pay for more hosting horsepower than you need

If you buy a hosting package and need to move to a larger package with more functionality, you can always upgrade later. If you start with a larger package and discover that you don't need it, you may not be able to back down to a smaller package.

If you are contacting web designers about a single website but have plans for additional websites, it helps to mention this, because your web designer will recommend a package that handles multiple websites. The cost of a package handling two or more websites is less than twice the cost of two single-website packages.

Log-Ins and Passwords

Keep close control over all of your log-in credentials

There are a number of log-ins that you will need to keep track of, including domain registration, hosting, e-commerce, newsletter, Google Analytics, PayPal, and social media. You can keep a spreadsheet, use a password-logging device on your computer, or keep a file just for website information. Whatever you do, keep track of the information.

Someone in your organization should be the master gatekeeper on all log-ins and passwords. Each piece of log-in information should only be given to those who really need to use it, and only on a case-by-case basis. And should an employee or contractor be terminated, you need to immediately know which items that person had access to so that they can be changed.

Assuming you have hired a web designer that you trust, there should be no problem with giving this person your log-in credentials. He or she will need access to everything involved with your website.

Some web designers, upon being hired, will give the new client a form or questionnaire to complete in order to gather the necessary log-in information. Be prepared before they ask for it.

If you give log-ins to multiple people, make sure you know who has which ones. In some cases, depending on the application, you may be able to create unique log-ins and passwords for each person who needs access. If you do that and have to replace someone or cut off access, you only have to disable one log-in.

Know how to remove access to all of your accounts

If you need to replace your web designer, make sure you know how to remove access to the website and all administrative or control panels.

Many web designers have a strong policy about access. If the initial invoices are still outstanding, the web designer may not give some log-ins to the client until he or she is paid. If the client does not pay bills on time, the designer easily has the ability to shut the website down in a matter of minutes. Most designers rarely have to use this approach, but it happens. The easy rationalization is that if the client has not paid for the work, the designer owns the website and can do whatever he or she wants with it, including shutting it down.

Your web designer is not your password backup system

While your web designer will have all or some of your log-ins, don't depend on that person to be your backup system. Make sure you have the information in your files. You may need the information when your web designer is not available, or you may need to remove your designer's access.

A client once contacted me with an urgent request. A member of his staff had been terminated, and she had the password to a general e-mail address used by the business. However, the business owner could not find the password and therefore could not log in to change it. It was all sorted out quickly, but relying on me for that password was not the best backup plan under the circumstances.

Have a trusted resource who can access your log-in information if something should happen to you

Someone else in your organization should know how to access all log-ins. If your organization has more than one employee, then a backup within the organization makes sense. However, if you're a solo practitioner, you should identify a backup resource who can access the information if you are unavailable (whether you are out of town, admitted to the hospital, or involved in some other kind of emergency).

Your backup could be your attorney, financial advisor, a member of your family—it matters less what the person's role is and more that it is someone you trust who is likely to know immediately if some stroke of bad fortune makes you unavailable.

In the last year, I had the sad situation of three clients passing away. In two cases, the client was involved in a family business, and other family members were there to pick up the ball when it came to business operations. Even so, they relied on me to reset passwords to e-mail accounts and to deal with other administrative details.

In the other case, a client was the victim of a tragic accident. Although he lived four hundred miles from me, we were long-time friends and communicated frequently by phone and e-mail, so I was aware of his business happenings. At the time, he had just cemented a partnership with another business owner. Unfortunately, the owner had no idea who or where I was. Fortunately, I was able to find him via social media. Imagine the relief of the person on the other end of the message—he had no idea who to contact about updating the website to change phone numbers, contact information, and other key data. We quickly had everything sorted out and handed over, but had I not been aware of the situation, it could have been a problem for him.

Follow password best practices and guidelines

There is no shortage of information available regarding best practices of password creation. Just in case you need some reminders, here are a few recommendations.

Do:

- Use special characters, such as nonalphabetic characters.

- Create passwords with at least eight characters.

- Use a password vault application to protect and help manage your many passwords.

- Change your most critical passwords on a regular basis.

- Have a strategy, formula, or algorithm to create passwords.

Don't:

- Use personal identifiable information in your password, such as names, birthday, pet's names, children's names, hobbies, or your school or alma mater.

- Use a single dictionary word as your full password.

- Use the same password for online banking that you use for social networking or e-mail.

- Give your password to someone over the phone.

- Use the same password everywhere.

Exercise: Log-ins and passwords

If you already have a website, you should have at least some of these log-ins. If you don't have a website yet, you can skip this step. For each item, know the name of the service provider, the link to the log-in page, the log-in, and password. Your web designer will confirm which ones are needed from you.

- ☐ registrar
- ☐ hosting
- ☐ blog
- ☐ Google Analytics or other statistics package
- ☐ newsletter
- ☐ content management system (CMS)
- ☐ e-commerce platform
- ☐ payment system (for your clients)
- ☐ e-mail
- ☐ Facebook (page link, plus log-in and password if your web designer will need to update or edit)
- ☐ LinkedIn
- ☐ Twitter
- ☐ other: _____

In Summary

- You may think it's about the tools, but web design is first and foremost a *process*.

- Effective web design extends far beyond integrating words and pictures into a visible page.

- Pay for the skills of a trained and experienced web professional, and free yourself to be an expert in your own field.

- Do it yourself to save money—but at the expense of results, functionality, and productivity.

- Hire a web designer for a more professional result, but expect to spend more.

Web Designers and Developers

- The terms *web designer* and *web developer* are often used interchangeably, but they are not necessarily the same.

- For many smaller organizations, it makes sense to find one resource to handle both design and development.

- Determine whether you will best be served by working with a company or an individual.

- When working with an inexperienced web designer, supervise vigilantly, and demand course correction immediately.

- Don't hire a family member—unless he or she is, in fact, a web designer

- No single web designer is a specialist in all aspects of design and development.

- Web design and print design require different skills.

- Web designers only *seem* to be online 24-7.

- Web design is not generally a nine-to-five office job.

- Identify a reliable tech support resource other than your web designer.

Website Mechanical Components

- Register your domain with a reputable and accredited registrar.

- Don't select your domain registrar based on price.

- It can be difficult to change domain name ownership once it's been established.

- Select a well-known hosting company with a stellar reputation for technical support.

- Keep an eye on the ever-shrinking cost of hosting.

- You can defer purchase of the hosting package until after hiring a web designer.

- Don't pay for more hosting horsepower than you need.

Log-Ins and Passwords

- Keep close control over all of your log-in credentials.

- Know how to remove access to all of your accounts.

- Your web designer is not your password backup system.

- Have a trusted resource who can access your log-in information if something should happen to you.

- Follow password best practices and guidelines.

PART 2
Do Your Homework

Pinpoint budget and timeline constraints. Do your prework by gathering information, conducting competitive analysis, identifying your audience, and drafting a marketing plan.

What do you think you could have done differently to reduce the cost?

"I wish my company was better organized at that time so content for the web pages was easier to collect."

"We should have had our homework done ahead of time so the designer wasn't waiting on us. There should be a consultation with 'homework' before ever starting. Once you start, time is ticking."

"I had no real way to compare what I was shopping for in choosing a web designer. Other than looking at samples of their work, I was more or less in the dark."

"I wish I would have known more about the range of rates. The quotes that I received varied by thousands of dollars, and it was not something that I expected."

"I wish we hadn't started until we had time free to work on it. It isn't something you just hand off to someone."

"Try not to change direction in the middle of the project."

—Survey responses

Website Prework

Your website is not just about who you are today but who you will be in one to three years

Before making a commitment, candidate web designers need key information to determine if your project is right for their skills and services. It all starts with who you are and what you do.

In just a couple of sentences, who are you? What product or service does your organization sell or provide? How long have you been in business? Where do you want your organization to go? What do you see for the future? What are your plans for growth or expansion?

Your website needs to reflect your goals and visions and should be able to grow with your organization. So if you're currently selling three products but plan to expand to twenty products in the next year, the candidate web designer needs to know that. This information is necessary to propose a solution that can handle today's needs as well as those required a year from now.

What is your mission? Your mission is simply a statement of the purpose of your organization, its reason for existing. It defines your key market, the contribution you make to that market, and the factors that distinguish you from the competition.

Your mission statement should also be a philosophy that guides the actions of the organization, influences goals, provides a path for actions, establishes a framework in which strategies are developed and executed, and can help guide both short- and long-term decision making.

What is your vision? Where do you expect your organization to be in one year? Three years? If your organization changes substantially over the next three years, it will probably be time to consider a website redesign.

Exercise: Who are we now, and who will we be in the future?

A two- to three-sentence description of our organization:

Our mission statement:

A vision of our organization in one year:

A vision of our organization in three years:

The products and services we provide now:

The products and services we will provide in one year:

The products and services we will provide in three years:

Know why you need a website before creating one

Every website should have a purpose—or possibly multiple purposes. Some reasons an individual, business, or organization might want or need a website are:

- to establish and demonstrate expertise

- to build credentials or a reputation

- to sell a product or service online

- to offer a free or subsidized product or service online

- to provide technical support

- to provide a knowledge base for customers

- to share opinions

- to provide detailed expertise on a personal interest

- to provide education on a specific topic or area of expertise

- to solicit donations that allow an organization to continue its work

- to raise money to fund a project

- to solicit volunteers

- to encourage participation in free classes, seminars, or events

- to accept registration and payment for classes, seminars, or events

- to document an event in progress with an end date (such as a political campaign)

- to solicit event sponsors or donations

Exercise: What is the purpose of our website?

The purpose of our website is to:

☐ demonstrate expertise

☐ establish credentials

☐ build reputation

☐ provide general information about our organization

☐ provide information about our products and services

☐ provide customer support

☐ provide technical support

☐ share opinions or editorials

☐ share personal interests

☐ share expertise on a topic

☐ share information in an educational way

☐ generate leads and inquiries

☐ generate revenue by selling a product

☐ generate revenue by selling a service

☐ provide a free product

☐ provide a free service

☐ solicit contributions or donations

☐ solicit volunteers

☐ engage participation in a free event

☐ engage participation in a paid event

☐ other: _____

Quantify your website's measurable objectives

The objectives of your website are different from the purpose. The *purpose* is the reason the website exists, whereas the *objectives* are the measurable results you expect to achieve with the website. Typically, a measurable item will be either an increase or decrease in some numerical quantity—or it may be an increase in the quality of some aspect of your business. The important point is to know how you will measure the success of the website.

Exercise: What are the objectives of our website?

The results we hope and expect to achieve with our website are to:

- ☐ introduce more people to our organization
- ☐ educate more people about this type of organization
- ☐ educate more people about a topic or area of expertise
- ☐ increase sales or orders of products or services
- ☐ increase the number of inquiries from potential customers or clients
- ☐ increase brand recognition
- ☐ increase our customer base
- ☐ increase donations
- ☐ increase volunteers
- ☐ provide the latest information about products and services to more potential customers or clients
- ☐ provide the latest information about products and services to current customers or clients
- ☐ increase event registrations
- ☐ increase event participation
- ☐ increase event sponsorship or funding
- ☐ other: _____

Realize and articulate what distinguishes you from the competition

The aspects that make your organization special could relate to the product or service you provide or the way in which you provide it. Certainly any distinguishing characteristic or advantage should be advertised on your website.

For example:

- Your product is unique, has the highest performance, lowest cost, or best quality.

- Your service is provided with the best quality, experience, knowledge, communication, responsiveness, thoroughness, reliability, or cleanliness.

- Your staff has the most advanced credentials, training, or experience.

- If similar products or services have negative stereotypes associated with them, you may need to show how your product or service does not fit those stereotypes.

Exercise: What puts us above the competition?

Our advantages over competitors are:

Our organization is differentiated by:

We are better than the competition because:

Our products or services are better than the competition because:

Clients or customers choose us over competitors because:

Connect with your audience by communicating your values

In addition to factual information about products and services, your website should communicate your values in a way that resonates and connects with visitors. Your values may apply to the attributes or personality traits of your organization or to a desired presentation format based on your target audience.

While a potential client may not realize it, when a client sees information on your website, it has the possibility to resonate with something he or she cares about. Everyone forms opinions when they see a website, whether or not they realize it as a strong positive or negative feeling.

Exercise: What are the values we want to communicate on our website?

The values we want to communicate on our website:

- ☐ feminine

- ☐ masculine

- ☐ youthful

- ☐ mature

- ☐ experienced

- ☐ conservative

- ☐ liberal

- ☐ devout or religious

- ☐ luxury or high-end quality

- ☐ economical or low price

- ☐ modern and up-to-date

- ☐ hands-on or involved

- ☐ hands-off or remote

- ☐ classic

- ☐ playful

- ☐ whimsical

☐ humorous

☐ satirical

☐ serious

☐ simple

☐ complex

☐ subtle

☐ obvious

☐ other: _____

Branding communicates values as well

If you have a logo and color scheme as part of your organization's branding, your web designer will need the files and information before any design work is started. If you do not have a logo or color scheme identified, this may be part of the overall website project or possibly a project to be completed before the website.

Color choices communicate more than you may assume. The colors used on your website may also communicate values to your audience. So while you might choose colors that appeal to you personally, it makes sense to deliberately select colors that have meaning, that convey a specific message to your audience, and that have a purpose in providing a feeling or emotion you wish to present. Some examples:

Red: energy, strength, power, passion, excitement, courage, risk, love, attention, bravery, emergency, crisis, anger, rage, aggression, violence

Pink: romance, love, friendship, truth, peace, calm, caring, nurturing, youth, femininity

Orange: sunshine, energy, happiness, childlike joy, warmth, vibrancy, excitement, endurance, encouragement, independence, ignorance, deceit

Yellow: intelligence, joy, brightness, happiness, optimism, learning, imagination, honor, warmth, caution, jealousy, criticism, betrayal, sickness, aging

Gold: wealth, winning, happiness, prestige, wisdom, concentration, caution, jealousy, criticism

Green: nature, healing, harmony, safety, ecology, physical healing, hope, tranquility, good luck, immortality, greed, money, jealousy, inexperience, ambition, cowardice

Blue: peace, calm, stability, trust, dependability, good fortune, wisdom, protection, reassurance, truth, sincerity, depth, experience, intellect, coldness, depression, passivity

Purple: sophistication, wealth, royalty, magic, creativity, spiritual power, enlightenment, dignity, independence, sadness, arrogance, conceit

Brown: earthiness, outdoors, inexpensive, enduring, stability, simplicity, comfort, generosity, fertility, practicality, boredom, conservatism

Black: elegance, power, sophistication, protection, formality, reliability, strength, prestige, modernism, mourning, grief, death, mystery, remorse, anger

White: purity, innocence, cleanliness, safety, spirituality, virginity, simplicity, youth, goodness, fairness, holiness, chastity, coldness, distance, harshness

Gray: security, reliability, modesty, dignity, maturity, conservatism, sophistication, durability, gloominess, sadness

Understand how your clients currently find you to know how your website can have an impact

If you already have a website, are you reaching potential clients via search results, referral links, ads, or some other method? You need data to know which methods are successful, which ones need to be improved, and which ones may require additional outside expenses.

If you do not already have a website, are you reaching potential customers or clients via advertising, personal referrals, or some other method? In some cases, having a website will enhance these approaches—such as listing your website in a print advertisement.

Exercise: How do clients find us now?

Currently, our clients find us through:

☐ referrals from current clients

☐ referrals from other business professionals

☐ referrals from friends or family

☐ phone book listing or advertising

☐ television or radio advertising

☐ print advertising

☐ flyers or posters posted locally

☐ links or articles on other websites

☐ local networking or business group activities

☐ speaking engagements or public appearances

☐ search engines

☐ social media references

☐ other: _____

Identify how you will attract website visitors

Rather than passively wait for people to find your website, drive them there proactively. Ideally you will have both online and offline sources of creating website traffic.

Every potential client tells me that they want to rank at the top in search engine results. This is a great goal to have, but it's sometimes an unrealistic one. This is not what you remember from the movie *Field of Dreams*, where they said, "If you build it, they will come." You will want a multifaceted approach to bring website visitors in from multiple directions and sources.

Exercise: How will we drive traffic to our website?

We will drive traffic to our website through:

- ☐ search engine results

- ☐ direct mail and marketing

- ☐ our marketing collateral items (coffee cups, pens, tradeshow giveaways)

- ☐ print advertising

- ☐ online advertising

- ☐ speaking engagements or public appearances

- ☐ magazine articles

- ☐ blog articles

- ☐ press releases

- ☐ social media

- ☐ signs posted at our place of business, visible to current clients

- ☐ signs outside our place of business, visible to passersby

- ☐ signs or magnets on vehicles

- ☐ referrals from friends or family

- ☐ referrals from current clients

- ☐ referrals from current participants

☐ referrals from business partners

☐ networking groups

☐ local chamber of commerce

☐ webinars

☐ e-books

☐ other: _____

Know how you will evaluate website success

Remember those objectives you identified earlier in this section? How will you measure whether or not these objectives have been achieved? You'll need to have an idea of your current performance—whether it's sales volume, inquiries, number of volunteers, or donation amounts. Even if you already have a website, you'll want to compare the results before and after the launch of your new website.

Exercise: How will we measure the success of our website?

We will measure success of our website by the:

- ☐ increase in calls or inquiries
- ☐ increase in number of visitors
- ☐ increase in frequency of website visits
- ☐ increase in sales
- ☐ increase in donations
- ☐ increase in registration and attendance at events
- ☐ increase in volunteers
- ☐ increase in referrals
- ☐ decrease in calls or inquiries for technical support
- ☐ increase in positive reviews
- ☐ decrease in negative reviews
- ☐ other: _____

Identify your desired audience by the qualities and traits that characterize its needs and values

Sometimes we forget who our target website audience really is, and it may very well be multiple audiences. For example, a doctor's office may have information on its website for new or potential patients, current patients, and referring physicians. A nonprofit organization's audiences could include service recipients, donors, and volunteers. For many websites, in addition to potential clients and customers, candidate employees may also be an important audience.

Your audience may not have requirements in each of these areas, but you should know which ones are relevant in order to ensure that your website appropriately addresses them.

Audiences may be characterized by attributes in one or more of these categories:

Physical: age, gender, health status

Cultural: race, religion, language, ethnic group, nationality, marital and family status

Personal: economic status, education level

Entity type: individual, small business, corporation, nonprofit organization, professional organization

Shared interest: skills, hobbies, leisure activities

Access method: type of system used to access the website (computer, tablet, smartphone, other), level of expertise using websites or associated applications, location of access (home, work, or public shared computer, such as library)

Relationship to website owner: current or potential customer, client, patient, supporter, employee, referral source

Exercise: Who is our audience?

Our primary target audience is characterized by:

Physical attributes:

Cultural attributes:

Personal attributes:

Entity type:

Shared interests:

Access method:

Relationship to website owner:

(Repeat for secondary or tertiary audiences as necessary.)

Define the *call to action* that you want your website visitors to take

The *call to action* is your invitation to website visitors to take the next step. It's a targeted suggestion to take action in a way that will bring you information, sales, prospective clients, donations, volunteers, or inquiries.

What is it that you want visitors to do? Is it to contact you for a free estimate? Should they review your portfolio? Buy your product? Download your e-book? Join your mailing list? Learn more about your area of expertise? Make an appointment? Register for your class? The possibilities are endless; you just need to know which ones apply in your case.

If you have multiple audiences, you probably have more than one call to action. For each audience, you should know what you want them to do first.

Exercise: What action do we want our website visitors to take?

After people visit our website, we want them to:

☐ contact us for a consultation

☐ buy a product

☐ buy a service

☐ download a document

☐ make a donation

☐ become a volunteer

☐ subscribe to our mailing list

☐ subscribe to our blog

☐ read an article

☐ register for a class, seminar, webinar, or event

☐ pay for a class, seminar, webinar, or event

☐ other: _____

Define a list of pages needed for your website, but let your web designer lead the architectural work

While your web designer will have some ideas about the pages needed for your website, you can prepare a list with your initial thoughts. Any web designer who is asked to provide a price estimate will need to know approximately how many pages are required for the website and the types of pages. Not all pages are created equally in terms of time and programming complexity.

It is not necessary to have an exhaustive list, but it helps define the scope, as well as the structure, of the website. Your web designer also needs to know which sections have multiple pages or subpages in order to plan the most effective navigation scheme.

Exercise: Which pages belong on our website?

☐ home

☐ about

☐ staff or team overview

☐ detailed individual pages for staff or team members

☐ history of the organization

☐ contact information

☐ contact form

☐ appointment request form

☐ feedback form

☐ map and directions

☐ employment information

☐ employment application

☐ open job and position details

☐ frequently asked questions

☐ policies

☐ specialties

☐ detailed pages for one or more specialties

☐ product overview

☐ detailed pages for one or more products

☐ service overview

☐ detailed pages for one or more services

☐ news

☐ current and upcoming events

☐ past events

☐ calendar or schedule

☐ donation information

☐ online donation form

☐ volunteer information

☐ volunteer application form

☐ privacy

☐ terms of use

☐ other disclosures required by some professions

☐ other: _____

Identify typical ongoing, regularly scheduled updates that will be required postlaunch

Of course you want to plan the frequency of your postlaunch updates and to account for them in your budget. In addition, your web designer will (or should) organize and present information based on how—and how often—it will be modified. If you plan to handle postlaunch maintenance yourself, that may also impact the implementation methodology chosen.

Exercise: Which ongoing updates will be required for our website?

Our website will need regular, ongoing updates for:

- ☐ coupons or discounts
- ☐ sales
- ☐ class calendar or schedule
- ☐ class registration
- ☐ event calendar or schedule
- ☐ event registration
- ☐ menus
- ☐ performance calendar or schedule
- ☐ ticket purchase
- ☐ newsletters
- ☐ regular column
- ☐ blog posts
- ☐ other:_____

Competitive Analysis

Take advantage of all that has been learned through development of existing websites, then make yours better

By reviewing other websites—both in your same market space and outside of it—you will realize what you like and don't like, generate new ideas, and discover innovative features you want to include on your website. In almost all cases, there are already websites for organizations or purposes similar to yours, so take advantage of their research and thinking.

There are very few truly new and unique ideas on most websites; the majority serve the same purpose and communicate information that is relevant to many types of organizations.

Even if you are selling a new and unique product or service, there are websites with similar features that can be learning tools. A few hours of recon work can uncover many ideas for you to consider. Most candidate web designers will immediately ask you for a list of other websites you have reviewed, as well as those of your competitors.

One of my favorite projects involved a medical clinic. In most cases, clients came to it via referral from their primary care physician. A number of recognized screening surveys were widely available, and the typical situation had patients completing the survey on paper (or perhaps printing the survey from a website and then completing it on paper). Following completion, a numerical score was assigned, and based on the score, the patient might be referred for screening or testing, along with a referral form provided by the primary care physician.

But this clinic wanted to take things a step further. Why stop at just posting the screening surveys online? The director's idea was to create an interactive version of the survey that the patient would complete online. Following completion, the website would produce a summary report, including all of the necessary information, which the patient could print, give to the referring physician to sign, and then make an appointment. The resulting report included the necessary information for the director.

Plagiarism is a no-no: use other websites as inspiration, but don't directly copy their content

Content is copyrighted, but the generic concept of a website feature is generally not. For example, the concept of a Frequently Asked Questions (FAQ) page is nothing new. The typical questions asked about your organization won't be new either. Specific answers to these questions written by others would be copyrighted (and might not even apply to your situation)—but you can be sure that the questions are generic and apply to multiple individuals, businesses, or organizations. Copying someone else's answer directly is plagiarism. If the same information applies to your business, take the time to write the answer in your own words, in a way that is relevant to your specific audience.

Review the style of other websites to clarify your likes or dislikes

It *is* all about you and your opinions. Candidate web designers will want to know what appeals to you and what you especially like or dislike about other websites. Even if you can't articulate *why* you like or dislike something, your gut instinct is still useful. Be on the lookout for aspects of other websites that you like, as well as those you don't like.

You can review other websites in these areas:

- *Style:* fonts, colors, graphics
- *Navigation:* location of navigation in the header or sidebar, nesting of multiple levels

- *Features:* slideshows, galleries, portfolios, videos, animation
- *Photos:* size, style, color space (color versus black-and-white), formatting (borders, shadows, frames), background versus all-white background
- *Pages:* layout, organization, cross-linkages
- *Titles and headings:* naming of pages, use of subheadings within pages

Exercise: Review local competitor websites

1. Name and website:

   Positive aspects:

   Negative aspects:

2. Name and website:

   Positive aspects:

   Negative aspects:

3. Name and website:

   Positive aspects:

   Negative aspects:

Exercise: Review websites of similar organizations that may not be local competition

1. Name and website:

   Positive aspects:

   Negative aspects:

2. Name and website:

   Positive aspects:

   Negative aspects:

3. Name and website:

   Positive aspects:

   Negative aspects:

Exercise: Identify websites you like

1. Name and website:

    Positive aspects:

    Negative aspects:

2. Name and website:

    Positive aspects:

    Negative aspects:

3. Name and website:

    Positive aspects:

    Negative aspects:

"First page Google results" is not necessarily a realistic feature request

Just about every potential client I speak with asks whether I can include SEO (search engine optimization) and guarantee that their website will appear on the first page of Google (or other search engine) results.

The answer is no.

As much as I want to guarantee results, there are many factors that go into search results, and only some of them are controlled by the person implementing the website. While optimizing search engine results is a reasonable objective, that single aspect requires a strategic plan composed of many elements. Some of these elements are controlled by the content provided by the client, while others can be programmed by the web designer. Yet others are influenced by factors outside of the actual website pages or programming. Each factor has some ability to be improved and used as well as possible, and each needs to be considered in turn.

As the client, it is your responsibility to influence those items under your control, to understand which items your web designer will handle, and then to work together to develop a plan to deal with the rest, as much as is feasible and practical.

For targeted SEO results, your best bet may be to hire an SEO specialist. Put this on your list of details to discuss with candidate web designers to find out what they can and cannot handle.

Some of the factors that enter into search engine ranking include:

- quality of content
- depth of content or significant substance
- the actual words used within the content
- the timeliness and freshness of the content
- the amount of real estate used for advertisement on the page

- the amount of time spent on the page once the visitor arrives there

- the titles and subtitles used in formatting the page

- other programmed tags that are part of the code but not visible to website visitors

- overall architecture and structure of the navigation

- management of duplication of content

- usability on mobile devices, such as smartphones and tablets

- quality and number of external websites that link or connect to the website

- length of time the domain and website have been available

- reputation on social networks, including rates of sharing of your content

- location of the website (country and locality)

- the speed at which website pages load

- meaningful page names (URLs) that include relevant keywords

There are also factors that can work negatively to decrease your website's overall ranking, including:

- paid or purchased links to your website

- creation of inbound inks via spamming, forums, or other means

- inclusion of pirated content

- hidden content that only appears to search engines and not human website visitors

- overuse of specific words that you feel will be likely search targets

- excessive use of advertisements

Timeline

Plan your launch schedule and timing to maximize financial and advertising opportunities

Financial

If you have financial constraints on your schedule, start the project early enough to spend the money within that time frame. If one of these scenarios applies to your project, candidate web designers need to know the details:

- You already have funding for the website, or it will be coming in the near future. This might be applicable to a nonprofit organization receiving grant funding or a start-up receiving investment funding.

- You are approaching the end of a budget cycle or fiscal year and want to include the website development fees during that period for budgetary or tax reasons.

Advertising and visibility

If there are opportunities coming that will provide visibility for your organization, start ahead of time so that the website is available for you to refer to at the time. If one of these scenarios applies to your project, candidate web designers need to know the details.

- One or more upcoming events will provide the opportunity to mention your website.

- A hard opening date has been scheduled, such as a ribbon-cutting ceremony or a grand opening event.

- Your organization will be receiving publicity, such as an award, a newspaper or magazine article, an interview, or other media event.

- Print materials listing the website are already being distributed or will soon be distributed

Exercise: Identify the items driving the launch date of our website

☐ A member of our organization will be speaking or featured at an event.

Date:

☐ We have a grand opening or ribbon-cutting scheduled.

Date:

☐ We will be receiving publicity on television or radio.

Date:

☐ We will be receiving publicity in print.

Date:

☐ We will be receiving publicity on another website.

Date:

☐ Our organization or a member of our organization will be receiving an award.

Date:

☐ Website funding is available and must be spent before a specific calendar deadline, based on the funding source's requirements.

Date:

☐ Website funding must be spent before the end of a budget cycle or fiscal year.

Date:

Set a hard deadline to encourage participant productivity

A defined deadline motivates both the client and the web designer to work quickly and provide timely feedback. It will also enable the web designer to do his or her job with minimal interference, because there is little time to waste.

Without a deadline, it's possible that the project will be reprioritized or trumped by other items that do have one.

While the web designer may not have lost money, as he or she was paid for work completed, there is also the frustration that comes with having the project hanging over his or her head, not knowing when the client will come back and suddenly demanding completion at a time that may or may not be convenient or realistic for the web designer.

In my case, when a project is delayed or put on hold, it also can potentially impact or jeopardize a future project. If I have allocated time in my schedule for a project with a set launch date and have also allocated future time to the next project, everything must be adjusted when the first project is delayed. Sometimes the first project will then have to be further delayed behind the next committed project—it's not fair to punish the upcoming project because the first client is behind schedule!

Total worked hours on a website project are never consecutive, but you can minimize delay time between the worked hours

If you are quoted 18 hours to complete a website project, those hours will not be completed in two consecutive nine-hour days, or even three consecutive six-hour days. Instead, work will be done in small batches, with frequent pauses for feedback.

It is certainly possible to complete a ten- or twenty-hour project in just a few days when the timing is critical, the client has a firm deadline constrained by outside events, and all needed materials are available. However, the more realistic timeline for a ten- to twenty-hour project is several weeks, assuming all parties can respond to questions and make decisions quickly.

One drawback of extended projects is that both the web designer and the client forget what was discussed, which decisions were made, and where they were in the process. A long break mid-project requires more time for everyone to reengage and get back up to speed. Some web designers will charge for this additional time.

Avoid being the critical path to completion of your website

Your web designer might work two to three hours, send you questions or a request for feedback, then wait hours, days, or weeks for your response before proceeding. Your web designer may not be able to move ahead until your response is received. Then he or she works another two to three hours and waits for another response. Your delay in response becomes the driving factor in the schedule.

Complete your preparation and recon work before beginning the hiring process

Save time and money by preparing as much as possible in advance and by committing to provide quick turnaround and feedback.

If your homework is done in advance, there is no delay after hiring, and your web designer is able to get started immediately. If you don't have the prework done, you may hire someone and then immediately put him or her on hold while you do that work. Any web designer you hire will want to review all of your prework and may ask for more, but you will have a big head start if you complete all or some of the exercises in Part 2.

Putting a website project on hold—for any reason—can increase the overall time worked in addition to the elapsed project time

Every web designer has a story about working on a twenty-hour project that spanned eighteen months. Projects are put on hold, and then the client is silent for months. Sometimes there is a legitimate reason to temporarily suspend a project, such as a major rebranding exercise or staffing change. And it's possible this won't be discovered until the project has been partially completed. If this happens, let your web designer know as soon as possible so that he or she can schedule accordingly.

Starting a major website project before an extended break can increase the overall timeline by longer than the actual elapsed time of the break

Starting a new website project shortly before Thanksgiving or the winter holiday season is challenging unless everyone is willing to commit to speedy responses. Otherwise, the project is partially completed, put on hold for a week or two, and then pushed later on the list after the January back-to-work frenzy. For this reason, some web designers will not agree to start a new project just before the holidays or before their own vacation.

Similarly, it would make sense to avoid starting a website project just before a long vacation, a wedding, maternity leave, an especially busy period for your organization, or any other major event that will demand your full attention away from the website project.

One mid-December evening, I received a frantic e-mail from someone in crisis: her new business was set to debut in January, and she'd widely publicized her new website, which she planned to have available on January 1. After several months of work, the web designer had flaked out, with no website in sight. She found me through referral, and although I discouraged her from starting a new project just before the holiday break, she felt she had no choice.

I agreed to start the project, and we hustled over the next week to start over and build the website. But as was to be expected, she was distracted with other holiday business and was unable to provide what I needed in order to complete the website before January 1. While I was willing to work during the expected holiday break, she was not able to give me what I needed, and the project slipped to her back burner for several weeks. The website was not completed until February because she was too busy getting her business launched.

Try starting your website project in late spring or midsummer

The most popular times to start new website projects are January, September, and November. Knowing this, it makes sense to avoid them in order to avoid competing with the web designer's busiest workload.

January brings out the people motivated to start the year with new plans and projects and the New Year's resolution folks.

September marks the end of summer vacation, the kids are back to school, and the weather is turning to fall, when more people are willing to get serious about getting back to work.

November and upcoming holiday season marketing reminds people that the year-end is suddenly right around the corner. If they want to deduct the cost of the website on this year's taxes, they need to get going with the project.

Every year I see a lull of activity in May as clients get busy with upcoming graduations, vacation planning, and the end of the school year. While I may be happy to see a slower work pace during the summer, I also have more time available to start new projects. Once September rolls around, I'm suddenly deluged with new projects.

Pricing

Hourly pricing protects the web designer from client inefficiency and enables clients to control costs

Hourly pricing (also referred to as *time and materials*) is a common form of pricing used by freelancers in many fields. You may have experienced this method in previous work with law firms, accounting firms, or design agencies. The client is billed at regular, predetermined intervals for the number of hours actually worked during that time interval by the person hired. Invoices might also include expenses for travel or items purchased on behalf of the client, such as stock photography, fonts, licensing for applications, or special software. If an increased project scope is requested, the web designer can estimate the additional hours required, and the client can decide whether the work should be done at that time. Hourly billing works best if the web designer is diligent about tracking work and is disciplined in being efficient.

- Clients like hourly pricing if there is a cap on the maximum number of hours and if they have the ability to reduce costs by handling some tasks on their own.

- Web designers like hourly pricing because they are protected if clients ask for additional out-of-scope work or repeatedly waste time with unnecessary or avoidable rework.

Fixed-fee pricing sets an upper limit to your cost and lets the web designer predict client billing

With fixed-fee pricing, the client is charged a flat rate for a service, project, or a series of related services or projects. The person doing the work is basing the cost estimate on his or her experience with similar projects. With experience, he or she should be proficient at getting close to the correct number in terms of getting paid for the hours worked, without overcharging. Even with fixed-fee pricing, if the client requests a scope change, the fee may be increased to cover the additional work. The risk in this arrangement usually falls on the web designer. An error in creating the estimate, or a client who requests multiple changes or revisions, could throw the time investment far beyond what was expected. Having a conversation about this could be awkward, if the client does not recognize his or her own behavior as the cause of the extra time.

- Clients like fixed-fee pricing because they know there is a set upper limit to the project cost and can plan accordingly.

- Web designers like fixed-fee pricing because they can predict their billing and know exactly how much they will be earning for the project.

Retainers work well if the client has an ongoing need for work on a regular basis and it provides reliable, steady income for designers

A retainer can be especially effective if the workload is fairly consistent, with approximately the same number of billable hours per billing period. The retainer is usually paid in advance or at regular billing periods throughout the year. A retainer can be considered an advance reservation for the designer's time, and is most likely to be a solution when there is already a good long-term relationship between the client and the web designer.

- Clients like knowing that time is reserved for their needs and that their designer is available, at a predictable cost.

- Web designers like retainers because they guarantee a reliable income stream on a steady basis. This also provides an environment of increased flexibility, as it allows the designer to do work without having to confirm every ten-minute request with the client.

Web designers can't be the best and the cheapest at the same time

While it is reasonable (and highly recommended) to request and receive a cost proposal on any new project, some web designers are not willing to write a competitive proposal and bid against other designers when the objective is to find the absolute lowest price.

If your goal is to compare proposals based on approach, thoroughness, and attention to detail, that's reasonable. However, if the purpose of a bidding war is to find the lowest cost, some designers will choose not to participate. An experienced and professional web designer does not expect to be the least expensive alternative and will not sandbag the estimate just to get the job.

Select the web designer who offers the best product for the cost you can afford, in the time frame you need

You can certainly shop around for a web designer and go with the one who offers the lowest price. If you have a very limited budget, you will need to acknowledge that early in the process. If you're entering into a competitive bidding process, let the participants know this. Some designers are unwilling to lowball their pricing just to get any project at all and will choose not to participate.

If you have a limited budget, you may not be able to afford a more experienced designer. In that case, you have the option of hiring someone with less experience or someone new to the business who is interested in building up a portfolio of work samples.

If you are in a hurry to have your website, you may have to compromise based on which designers are available. Popular web designers with a strong track record can be booked up months in advance and are simply unavailable for a new project in a short time frame. Web designers already maintaining a large group of existing websites may have limited capacity to take on new design projects.

Don't fall for an unbelievably low initial price quote

If a candidate web designer quotes a price that seems unbelievably low, watch out. It's possible that any of the following situations may apply:

- The quote is based on hard constraints, such as a set number of pages or the exclusion of key features.

- The scope of the project may not include everything you would like to have on your website.

- The fee may include basic design and programming but no content development or search engine optimization.

- The designer may be inexperienced.

- It may be a bait-and-switch approach—where the quoted cost gets the initial website going, but then every additional item jacks up the price.

Don't expect a price break based on promised referrals or word-of-mouth advertising

Referrals should be based on the web designer doing a good (great, fabulous, amazing) job and being well worth the investment. It's unrealistic to promise the referral of new business if a client has not received that designer's completed work and evaluated it to be an excellent product. If a client is given a discount in exchange for advertising, the people he or she refers may know about it and could expect the same discount. In addition, there is no way for the designer to hold the client accountable to this promise and no way to verify delivery upon it.

Several years ago, I was approached by a woman who was establishing a local nonprofit agency to provide a much-needed service. We had the standard initial conversation so I could learn more about the organization and the needs of the website. When it came time to talk about the budget, she said she had no money for a website at all and was counting on me to support her cause with completely pro bono work. She volunteered that by way of payment she would promise to spread the word about my wonderful work (mind you, she had not actually seen any my wonderful work on her behalf at that point) and send lots of referral work my way.

While I have taken on a number of free or discounted projects for worthy causes, I don't do it based on an expectation of referrals. For one thing, she might very well be unhappy with my work and not follow through. And then where am I? No payment, no referrals. In addition, I don't really want to do work on a pro bono basis and then have someone spread the word that I'm doing free work.

While I respected her desire to start the nonprofit organization, it is no one's responsibility but hers to secure funding for the proper business requirements. Had she been able to find funding at any level, I might have been willing to offer a substantial discount. It turns out that even when clients are receiving a huge discount, if they are paying by the hour, they are still more respectful of the web designer's time.

At the time, I politely declined, but she kept pressuring me with subsequent phone calls and e-mails about how much she admired my work and wanted me to be involved. Eventually I gave in and agreed to work on the website—but with the caveat that she trust me to do the work efficiently and without too much interference, given that I was volunteering my time. She agreed, but within two weeks it was clear that she was micromanaging me and monopolizing far too much of my time. I had to bow out of the project and let her find another resource. Even the promise of future referrals was not worth the aggravation.

Website projects can't be addressed with a generic "one-size-fits-all" pricing model

You may have based your cost expectations on reading an article, seeing a package offered by another web designer, or talking to a friend who paid that amount. There is no article, standard price, or any other system that will tell you the exact amount you should be paying for your website. This situation is nothing like the price competition between two stores for the same brand of TV set. No two websites are the same. Your candidate web designer needs to know how you arrived at this preconceived price so that you can discuss any unrealistic expectations and possible options to address them.

Website pricing is not necessarily an offer and counteroffer situation

Imagine going into a store and offering a lower price for an item than what is marked. You don't expect to walk into the local coffee shop and say, "I'm only willing to spend two dollars for that drink that normally costs three fifty."

When a price is quoted, a better approach is to ask about any trade-offs that might lower the price. Trade-offs could include the client handling some tasks that don't require the web designer's experience. They could also include trusting the web designer to make decisions without additional negotiation or discussion time. An experienced web designer will have suggestions that might enable a lower cost, with compromises. However, if he or she is willing to offer or counter, with no change in deliverables, quality or schedule—it means that the designer's original price was higher than necessary, and he or she was fishing for a higher profit than deserved.

I was once contacted by a local software start-up who was anxious to get its website established. I met with the owner, we discussed the project and objectives, and I wrote a proposal. His response was that my pricing was far too expensive and that he could find much cheaper programming resources overseas, so I should be offering a lower price. In fact, it turned out that his own programming resources for the start-up were overseas.

My first question was to wonder why he was seeking a local web designer in the first place. It turned out that the name of the business was connected with a local historical landmark, and he wanted to clearly give the impression that it was located in this community (which would be a marketing plus when approaching potential clients). But then the work would all be done overseas—where it was cheaper! And he'd figured out that he needed someone with knowledge around local marketing, networking, and community information. Surely the programmers in another country (no matter how technically brilliant) would not be of use in that case.

While it's reasonable to think that a web designer might offer a discount to organizations at their discretion, it's not at all realistic to think that one would offer a discount just to compete with cheaper resources in another country. The right perspective is that the pricing should reflect the value offered and the local competitive pricing for the product. So what might be purchased overseas could very well be the same programming quality, but not the same design, content, editing, or presentation needed.

Cash offers are insulting (and illegal)

Treat this like the legitimate business engagement that it is. Assume your web designer will declare their income and assume that your organization will declare the fees as a business expense.

A potential client once offered to pay me with cash, in exchange for a discount. His rationale was that I would not have to pay taxes on the income, since I was paid in cash. He thought I could avoid declaring it and save the taxes. The flaw in his logic was that he would pay less that way, but I would keep the same amount of money (not to mention that it's illegal to not declare the income). I turned down his offer and said I would only accept the original terms of engagement, as per my proposal. We did the project, but I was constantly on the lookout for some other suggestion from him to do something illegal or unethical. In the end, his business venture lasted about a year, and then he was on to something else, so I was off the hook.

A good cause is not justification to request pro bono work

It's unreasonable to think that every contractor or business can donate time or services just because the recipient is a nonprofit organization. I get it: there are many nonprofit organizations with limited budgets. And they will certainly find a variety of ways for supporters to donate money or goods.

However, many web designers refuse to take on pro bono work, simply because there is less value placed on uncompensated or unpaid work. The worker is treated as a volunteer, and yet the demands are often the same as for a paid employee or contractor. When changes are requested, the expectation is still that they will be completed as quickly as possible and with the same expectation of high quality. There's no accountability as to how much time was actually spent—whereas an invoice would show actual billable hours.

And don't even suggest that the web designer can take a tax deduction for offering the pro bono work—that's not true. On the other hand, if the web designer pays some fees that the organization would otherwise pay (such as domain registration or hosting), those fees could be considered a financial contribution to the organization. The volunteer web designer may also be able to deduct local travel expenses, telephone expenses, or parking fees if the expenses were part of managing the website.

It's possible that discounts will be offered to nonprofits in exchange for other considerations, such as advertisement as an in-kind sponsor. This advertisement could be in the form of a credit on the website, an ad in printed material (such as an event program), or some other public form of recognition. Even if the billable rate is a small percentage of the normal rate, there is visibility into the work done and the time spent.

If you're paying anything lower than full price, be prepared to wait in line

You may be receiving a discount for any number of reasons: you could be a nonprofit organization, a friend of the web designer, a business partner, or a member of a professional organization. In any case, if you are receiving a price break, be prepared to wait a bit longer for your requests to be handled. Clients paying full price deserve to be placed higher on the list than those who are not.

In the case of completely free or donated work, a pro bono project will have to take last priority behind billable work, as well as discounted work, especially if the web designer is in demand or has a large established client base.

What this means for you: plan ahead even further.

If you are lucky enough to actually find a volunteer, treat that person like gold

Should you be fortunate enough to find a willing, able, and competent volunteer to design or manage your website, thank that person every chance you get. It is not surprising that some of my favorite volunteer projects are for the ones who actually say thank you. A simple note, a listing as an in-kind donor or sponsor in an event program, or the occasional testimonial on social media all do wonders for the attitude of the web designer.

I never expect gifts from clients (pro bono or otherwise), but when a pro bono client takes the time to send me a token gift card for ten dollars at the local coffee shop, or drop by with a bottle of wine, it reminds me that he or she really *does* care about my contribution. The effort speaks volumes and renews my dedication to the client's cause.

Then again, be careful with your public thanks. After I designed the website for a local nonprofit organization at no cost, the executive director placed an advertisement in the local paper: "Thanks to Collective Discovery for providing free websites for community nonprofits." Needless to say, my phone started ringing off the hook, as others got excited about the prospect of a free website. Sometimes too much public thankfulness is not a good thing. Private thanks are just fine!

Save money by delegating tasks that don't require your web designer's skills

A professional web designer has the skills to do everything associated with building the website. However, you may also find yourself asking the designer to take on tasks that you can do on your own—or delegate to others, including employees or volunteers. These tasks include:

- data entry

- retyping print items

- proofreading draft copy

- searching through stock libraries for photos

When interviewing candidate designers, ask if they have suggestions for tasks that clients can take on to save money.

The bad behavior of "clueless clients" adds to the project cost

In the web designer's world, a "clueless client" is one who abuses the process, the work, and the relationship, generally through his or her own thoughtless or poorly considered behavior.

If a client repeatedly misbehaves or abuses the web designer, he or she runs the risk of being charged more, or even dropped. These choices and behaviors typically result in taking more of the web designer's time or forcing rework due to lack of planning. In some cases, they lead to conflict between the work of the original web designer and someone else, with no clear identification of responsibility when arbitration or correction is required.

The following are behaviors that may get you labeled as a *clueless client*:

- Send requests for information or changes by text message or social media channels.

- Leave change requests on voice mail.

- Delay response to requests for information or clarification and leave your web designer on hold long enough that he or she needs to confirm whether you even received a message.

- Don't proofread materials before sending to your web designer.

- Allow multiple people to submit instructions or feedback to the web designer without consolidation or discussion among the group.

- Give back-end access to other vendors or service providers without notifying your web designer.

- Hire and pay other vendors or service providers without first confirming whether your current web designer can provide those same services.

- Ask your web designer to do something illegal or unethical.

Budget

Understand your financial constraints, and plan your budget accordingly

Whether you already have a website or are considering creating one, if you don't have an in-depth understanding of your budget and plan accordingly, you *will* get surprised. In addition to the initial start-up expense of getting that website designed and making it available to the public, you'll need to allocate money for ongoing maintenance and for marketing of the website.

The care and feeding of your website is a necessary expense

A website is not an optional item or "extra" expense. If you see it that way, your website may fall short of your expectations. If your organization does not have a website, you are losing business to a competitor who does have one. It should be a required item in any marketing budget, and if you want to get the best possible value out of your initial investment, it should be considered an ongoing expense. Yes, that means spending money forever if you want to get the best return on your initial investment.

A website is a leveraged expense, staying available long after the money is spent

Once you have a website, it's there for as long as you pay the administrative costs. Even if you choose not to update it, that website is working for you, 24-7. When you place an ad in print or on the radio, it has a short shelf life after the initial publication (unless you continue to pay for placement).

Are you still spending money for ads in the local phone book? Is that your best source of potential customers or clients? We now know that more people look online than in a phone book. I'm not suggesting that you should stop advertising in the phone book—but you may opt for a smaller ad or advertise in fewer local directories. That saved money can be applied to the website.

Evaluate the return on each set of marketing materials, and prioritize the website launch timing relative to the other materials

It will be helpful for a candidate web designer to know about other marketing expenses you have planned. He or she may be able to help you reevaluate or coordinate the timing of various items, and deferring one other item for a few months could be enough to provide the funds for the website. For example, paying for a TV or print ad when you don't have a website yet may not be the optimal order of events. It would be better to have the website in place first and then drive website visitors through the ad.

As an example, a neighborhood franchise of a national company wanted to develop a local client base. The parent company did offer them a customized page on the corporate website, but they were limited in what could be done with their information. Their budget included a television advertisement that would be played locally, and we had already been discussing their options for a website but had not yet started the project.

They created the TV ad before we implemented the website, losing the opportunity to drive website traffic through the ad, although we were able to include the ad on their website when it was eventually developed. Ideally, the website would have been in place before the ad appeared, providing a logical next step for interested viewers of the ad.

Invest in frequent website updates to maintain usefulness and relevance, and include maintenance costs in your long-term budget

Once you have your website, your goal is to keep it fresh and current. A website is not a project that is done once and forgotten. Add new content that is of value to both new and returning visitors—encourage them to return and stay engaged. No updates means no need to come back.

Some organizations can manage ongoing updates on their own after the website has been launched. However, that's not always the case. If you take over maintenance of your website and accidentally break something, you may spend more paying an expert (your original web designer or someone else) to fix it than you would have paid in the first place to have the work done. In addition, there may be a negative impact if your website is down or displaying incorrect information for any length of time.

Some web designers charge a monthly retainer for maintenance, whether or not they are requested to make any changes. Other designers only charge if they are called on to do actual work on the website. Before you get to the maintenance stage, you'll need to know the terms on which that work will be done.

Some web designers will only take on maintenance work for websites they originally designed. Taking over maintenance on a website designed by someone else can be frustrating due to different programming styles, as well as the possibility that the first designer did a poor job, which requires additional attention to fix. If a web designer is not interested in handling maintenance work, you will need to find someone else to do it after the website is launched, or you should consider another designer.

If your website will require regular ongoing maintenance, a retainer system may be to your advantage.

Have the money available before starting your website project

You may not have all of the money in hand at the time you start the project, but you should expect that you will have to pay the bills before your website is launched (or shortly thereafter). Ideally, all of the funding is already in the bank or at your disposal. As Mom used to tell me, don't charge a purchase on your credit card if you don't already have that money in your checking account.

If you do not have complete website funding resources available, and you still want to work with a specific web designer, then the challenge is to find a way to make it work for both of you. If you're assuming that you have to come up with the entire amount up front before the project starts, that can possibly be addressed by progress payments or a payment plan. Some web designers will be willing to work with you on this.

Once you get started, the assumption is that you will be able to pay invoices at the time they arrive

A very frustrating client (former client, that is) was a women's networking organization. The organization hired me to create a website for a large luncheon award event happening in May. They contacted me just before Christmas, and if I had followed my own advice, I would have said the project could not be started until January. But they gave me a hard sell about how critical the website was to bringing in sponsors and attendees, and that marketing needed to start promptly on January 1. So I hustled over the holiday break, had the website about 80 percent completed and was waiting for their final content by January 1. For the entire month of January, I waited while they got their act together. Normally, I send invoices on the first of the month for work done during the previous month, but I was generous and let the project billing slide to February 1. By the time I sent that invoice, we still did not have the content to launch the website, and now I'd given them an interest-free loan for over a month. After several weeks, still no content, and still no payment. No worries for me: I simply said I would not complete and launch the website until receiving payment.

Imagine my surprise when I was told that they did not have the money to pay for the website yet—as they were still waiting to secure sponsors. And of course they could not really solicit sponsors without that website. At that point, I was no longer feeling quite so generous and said that if I did not receive payment for the work already delivered (over my holiday vacation, plus an interest-free loan), the website would not be launched. Eventually one of the committee members paid me with a personal check, and the organization owed the money to her. As soon as that website was completed and launched (in March), I bowed out, gave them the passwords, and said they were welcome to maintain it on their own through the event.

Cost, schedule, feature set: choose two out of three

It is unrealistic to constrain a time frame, budget, and feature set and assume that all three can be met. If you have a limited budget, that may influence what can be accomplished in your desired time frame.

Almost anything you want to do on your website is possible—if you have no constraints around time or money. In general, you can fix two of the three parameters, and that will define what is possible for the third. For example, if you have an absolute list of feature set requirements and a hard deadline for the website launch, candidate web designers will tell you what the pricing expectations must be. If you have a fixed budget and timeline, you may have to compromise on the feature set or other website performance requirements.

When you ask for a feature and your web designer says it's not possible, he or she may really be saying, "You can't afford this, based on your budget" or "It's not worth the investment, considering the effort versus return." So if you're told something is not possible, ask which parameters are driving that conclusion.

My recommendation is to identify the feature set and needs of the project as well as the time frame, then let the web designer tell you what cost is reasonable to expect. After that, if the cost is still too high (based on your budget or expectations), ask the web designer to help prioritize the project into a two-phase implementation, and determine which features can be deferred to a later enhancement of the website.

Possible sources for clients on a severely limited budget include relatives, students, and newcomers to the web design business

Every professional freelance web designer started his or her career building websites at no cost in order to create a portfolio of work samples. If you can find someone who is looking for just this opportunity, it could be a valid solution—with the caveat that you will not get the same results as you would by hiring (and paying) a pro. In fact, you may not get any results at all—but it could be worth a shot. For example, if you hire a student, you can reasonably guess that he or she may not be around long-term, after graduation.

One of my clients came to me after having hired a college student over the summer break. The student was enrolled at the client's alma mater (in fact, also my alma mater), and he thought it was a good situation, given their common commitment to the university. Sadly, he paid the student half of the fee up-front, and the project was not completed to the client's specification. The design looked nothing like the examples provided, and after months of waiting, he still did not have a finished website.

Once school started up again in September, the student was unavailable, and another resource had to be hired. Unfortunately, when I took over, the student's work was not reusable, and we started from scratch. In the end, my client had no way to recover his initial investment, and the student was let off the hook, with cash in his pocket.

What's the lesson? When hiring a student, you need to find a way to guarantee that he or she will be around and available to complete the project. Honestly, that situation might only happen when you are related to the student or somehow have a long-term relationship. One possible approach would be to set up a weekly schedule with deliverables, and at the first hint that the student cannot meet commitments, stop the project.

Build recurring annual administrative fees into your budget

Just as you pay annual fees to keep your car or personalized license plate registered with the state, you must pay annual fees to keep your website up and running. Typical recurring costs include:

- domain name registration (an annual fee, typically less than twenty dollars per year)

- website hosting (a monthly fee, often as low as five dollars per month if you pay for months or years at a time)

- optional domain fees, such as privacy controls (which limit the availability of your personal contact information in association with your domain)

While these costs are not large, they are also nonzero, so they need a place in your budget.

Avoid outsourced work that gets the middleman markup

It may be that your chosen web designer does not have the expertise needed, and reinforcement troops must be called in to complete some parts of the project.

Always ask whether any part of the project will be handed off to other individuals. Whether you pay them separately or not, there may be added cost as the originally hired person marks up his or her work.

A relative's friend hired a design firm in another state to design and build her website. When I volunteered to review the website and give feedback, I saw some disturbing issues, including the fact that the web designer had not corrected spelling and grammar errors in the content she provided. A bit of digging in the source code revealed that the programming had been outsourced to someone in another country (this was confirmed through comments in the code itself, with attribution). When I asked, the friend had no idea that the programming had been outsourced, which presented several issues:

- *The person she was in contact with had no direct involvement with the programming.*

- *The person doing the programming did not share a native language with the business owner.*

- *The web designer was probably marking up the cost of the programmer's work.*

- *The programmer was not receiving direct instructions from the client, so there was no discussion about correction and no feedback about the appropriate use of content.*

Rush projects cost more

In exchange for weekend or overnight work, or a reprioritization of the web designer's existing workload, a rush project may demand a premium, surplus charge, or bonus. A project requiring work on a holiday may also be charged extra. Then again, your web designer may love the challenge and adrenaline rush that comes with an all-nighter. To be honest, I prefer quick projects (even urgent weekend and night jobs) because we get the momentum going, produce quick and effective results, and get the project done with minimal interruption.

That being said, your web designer would like to spend nights and weekends enjoying his or her personal life—same as you! So if you're going to make extra demands that force abandonment of the designer's personal plans, he or she should be compensated.

Rush projects may force you to give up some creative control

While this is not a financial cost, it can be an emotional one. In exchange for the immediate turnaround on your project, you may pay the price by accepting whatever work can be provided in that shorter time frame.

One of my favorite rush jobs was a website for a local medical practice. Another major practice in town with the same specialty was moving to a new medical system. Given insurance constraints, many clients would not be able to move with them. So my client quickly set up several open house events for community members to meet their physicians—and their current website was in major need of upgrading to give the best possible impression. Ads in the local newspaper the next week would be listing their domain, yet it was not the image they hoped to present to this potentially large audience.

Given the timing, they had no choice but to trust me to do the design work in a vacuum, in order to produce a website over the weekend. Indeed, we met the deadline, had the new website up and running before the ad appeared, and all was well. Three years later, we did a complete redesign, and this time we followed the more standard process, where the client actually had a say in what the website looked like.

Expect to pay for other items in addition to the web designer's fees

Extra features will enhance functionality of your website and improve the end result. They will also add to the cost of the website. Some are costs for services that may not be part of the web designer's initial fee, unless you specifically ask about them. When you speak with candidate web designers, mention any items in this list to make sure they are included in the project scope and cost proposal.

Costs in addition to the fees charged by the web designer may include:

Branding

- design of a logo
- creation and selection of a color palette
- fonts used as part of your website design
- creation of print materials that may also be on the website (flyers, brochures, printable or fill-in ready forms)

Photography and video

- stock photography, illustration artwork, or video
- professional photographer or videographer
- professional models for a photo shoot

Additional features

- templates or themes used as part of the website design
- plug-ins, utilities, or services that provide additional functionality

- e-commerce processing fees (credit card processing fees, PayPal fees, fees charged by other e-commerce platforms)

- online registration systems for classes, camps, seminars, webinars, or events

- online donation systems

- newsletter or e-mail marketing systems

- additional security (which might be required for financial transactions or patient privacy)

Exercise: Identify basic staffing costs in addition to the website design

We will need additional help or staffing to:

- ☐ register a domain name
- ☐ find a hosting provider
- ☐ design a logo
- ☐ define a color palette
- ☐ design print materials
- ☐ take original photos of staff or our location
- ☐ create video
- ☐ write and edit content
- ☐ search for photos
- ☐ set up social media accounts
- ☐ identify vendors for off-site applications, such as payment or registration systems
- ☐ other:_____

Exercise: Identify features that add costs to your website

☐ flash or animation

☐ slideshows

☐ video

☐ blog

☐ membership registration

☐ event registration

☐ discussion forums or chat rooms

☐ news feeds

☐ online donations

☐ surveys or polls

☐ newsletters

☐ embedded calendars

☐ advertising integration

☐ e-commerce capabilities

☐ search engine optimization (SEO)

☐ links to social media websites

☐ custom design on social media websites

☐ forms (contact, appointment request, donation, etc.)

☐ photo gallery

☐ portfolio or gallery of work samples

☐ custom maps or diagrams

☐ members-only or password-protected areas for employees

☐ other:_____

In Summary

Website Prework

- Your website is not just about who you are today but who you will be in one to three years.

- Know why you need a website before creating one.

- Quantify your website's measurable objective.

- Realize and articulate what distinguishes you from the competition.

- Connect with your audience by communicating your values.

- Branding communicates values as well.

- Understand how your clients find you now in order to know how your website can have an impact.

- Identify how you will attract website visitors.

- Know how you will evaluate website success.

- Identify your desired audience by the qualities and traits that characterize its needs and values.

- Define the *call to action* that you want your website visitors to take.

- Define a list of pages needed for your website, but let your web designer lead the architectural work.

- Identify typical ongoing, regularly scheduled updates that will be required postlaunch.

Competitive Analysis

- Take advantage of all that has been learned through the development of existing websites, then make yours better.

- Plagiarism is a no-no: use other websites as inspiration, but don't directly copy their content.

- Review the style of other websites to clarify your likes or dislikes.

- "First page Google results" is not necessarily a realistic feature request.

Timeline

- Plan your launch schedule and timing to maximize financial and advertising opportunities.

- Set a hard deadline to encourage participant productivity.

- Total worked hours on a website project are never consecutive, but you can minimize delay time between the worked hours.

- Avoid being the critical path to the completion of your website.

- Complete your preparation and recon work before beginning the hiring process.

- Putting a website project on hold—for any reason—can increase the overall time worked in addition to the elapsed project time.

- Starting a major website project before an extended break can increase the overall timeline by longer than the actual elapsed time of the break.

- Try starting your website project in late spring or midsummer.

Pricing

- Hourly pricing protects the web designer from client inefficiency and enables clients to control costs.

- Fixed-fee pricing sets an upper limit to your cost and lets the web designer predict client billing.

- Retainers work well if the client has an ongoing need for work on a regular basis, and they provide reliable, steady income for designers.

- Web designers can't be the best and the cheapest at the same time.

- Select the web designer who offers the best product for the cost you can afford, in the time frame you need.

- Don't fall for an unbelievably low initial price quote.

- Don't expect a price break based on promised referrals or word-of-mouth advertising.

- Website projects can't be addressed with a generic "one- size-fits-all" pricing model.

- Website pricing is not necessarily an offer and counteroffer situation.

- Cash offers are insulting (and illegal).

- A good cause is not justification to request pro bono work.
- If you're paying anything lower than full price, be prepared to wait in line.
- If you are lucky enough to actually find a volunteer, treat that person like gold.
- Save money by delegating tasks that don't require your web designer's skills.
- The bad behavior of clueless clients adds to the project cost.

Budget

- Understand your financial constraints, and plan your budget accordingly.
- The care and feeding of your website is a necessary expense.
- A website is a leveraged expense, staying available long after the money is spent.
- Evaluate the return on each set of marketing materials and prioritize the website launch timing relative to the other materials.
- Invest in frequent website updates to maintain usefulness and relevance, and include maintenance costs in your long-term budget.
- Have the money available before starting your website project.
- Once you get started, the assumption is that you will be able to pay invoices at the time they arrive.
- Cost, schedule, feature set: choose two out of three.
- Possible sources for clients on a severely limited budget include

relatives, students, and newcomers to the web design business.

- Build recurring annual administrative fees into your budget.

- Avoid outsourced work that gets the middleman markup.

- Rush projects cost more.

- Rush projects may force you to give up some creative control.

- Expect to pay for other items in addition to the web designer's fees.

PART 3
Discovery

Search for qualified candidate web designers that fit your requirements. Initiate contact, complete the investigation and proposal process, and check references.

What do you think you could have done differently to shorten the timeline?

"Entered the project with a better idea of how we needed to utilize the site and what our maintenance challenges might be."

"With a better understanding of what we needed to do and what our options were, we may have been able to have more focused discussions and avoided trying something to discover it needed to be tweaked."

"More research from other sites to help with laying out elements for my website designer."

"Set myself clear limits prior to starting and during the process. It is hard to pull back once one is enthralled and involved with the process and product."

"Think long and hard about your product, what the message is you actually want to put out there, and figure out how to keep your message relevant, realistic, and useful."

"I should have cleared more time on my calendar and [the calendars of] those who were involved in decisions for the process."

—Survey responses

Finding Qualified Web Designers

You don't need to hire the first web designer you find

My grandmother always said, "Don't pick the first head of cabbage." I'm pretty sure she meant not to always grab the first opportunity that comes along, and don't marry the first guy you fall in love with. In other words, you don't have to go with the first web designer you meet or the first one you interview.

You don't need to find the single best web designer in the world, the country, or even the state. There are plenty of qualified web designers available and capable of delivering what you need. You just want to find the right one for you, and you have choices.

The best way to find a web designer is a recommendation from someone you trust

Use your network to find candidate web designers through contacts you already know and trust. A friend or business associate would not recommend a resource who reflects poorly on the original recommender. If your contact was unhappy with the work, it's unlikely that he or she would give a recommendation—in fact one might recommend that you do *not* hire a particular resource.

If you like the website of another local organization (presumably not your competitor), and you know the owner or an employee, ask if he or she would recommend the designer.

Don't rely only on the information on a web designer's website, which of course could be filled with anything one wants to say. You will get far more information from someone who has worked with this web designer.

Recommendations also reflect real-life experience in working with this web designer. While his or her finished work product is a good example of what the designer is capable of delivering, you want to be comfortable with this web designer's personal working style. It's easier to work with someone who is responsive, collaborative, flexible, and open-minded and who shares your sense of humor. Only another client can give you objective input on these attributes.

Find referrals through your local networking, business, or professional groups

If you are a member of a business networking group, professional organization, or service group, a web designer may also be a group member. If not, ask other group members for their recommendations. Many will have a website for their own organization, and some will have a web designer they recommend.

Another good resource is the website of the local chamber of commerce or business association. Even if you are not a member of the organization, its member directory is usually available on its website. A business that has made a commitment to join the local association or chamber has also made a long-term commitment to its community and will be more likely to stick around.

Post a query to a group discussion board or mailing list. This group or list might not even be related to your organization. It could be a parents' group or alumni community. The fact that your common interest has nothing to do with business or websites does not rule out the likelihood that someone else in the group has similar needs to yours when it comes to running one's own organization.

If you are a member of a professional association for your type of organization or service offering, there may be recommended vendors and suppliers, also possibly listed on the association's website. In fact, if you determine that the association's website was designed by a third party, that could be a great resource.

As an example, I manage the website of a state association representing a particular medical specialty. Some members of the association also became my clients, having found me from the design credit on the association's website.

I have also received numerous referrals via the alumni discussion forum from the university where I earned my master's degree. I don't advertise there, but occasionally a member posts a query, asking for referrals to local web designers (I live twenty miles from the school), and clients (also alumni) will post my name and website.

Look for the design credit as a referral source

Speaking of design credits, you can usually find one on a website designed by a professional. Most professional web designers will install a design credit and link somewhere on the website, as it's one way to substantiate their work. You are free to find websites for the businesses in your same market space locally and track down the web designers. In this case, no referral or personal introduction is required.

Hire a local web designer when possible

Working with someone local is best, whether you are the client or the web designer. Even if you can't find a local web designer that meets your requirements, there are plenty of web designers who work long-distance. However, it's a bigger risk to engage long-distance, so know your options and get references from other long-distance clients working with this web designer.

A local web designer knows the local landscape. If your marketing success is heavily dependent on local details and recognition, you want to work with someone who is familiar with your community and customer base. A local web designer will have a better understanding of your potential clients, local competition, likely marketing venues, and the subtleties of the geographic region (including local terminology).

For example, my hometown is included in a group of three cities known collectively as the Tri-City area. Just up the freeway a few miles is a group of three cities known as the Tri-Valley area. Clearly, advertising as one or the other will attract different clients. Anyone who does not live near here would not know about this nomenclature distinction.

A local web designer has the potential to be a great networking tool. A local web designer can bring you new clients, recommend relevant resources, and facilitate networking with possible business partners. If you're a nonprofit organization, your local web designer might also be a good connection to donors, volunteers, and contributors of auction prizes for your events.

A local web designer can meet with you in person. While it's not a requirement, it's a bonus if your web designer can visit your office or store, see your organization, meet with you to discuss plans or projects, and attend your events.

A local web designer is in your time zone, which allows the maximum overlap of typical working hours.

I'm in California and try to stick with only west coast clients, but when I had clients on the east coast, they would occasionally forget about the time difference, and I'd hear my cell phone ringing at 6:00 am. On the other end of the workday, I'd be hard at work at 3:00 pm, have a question, and realize that I could not reach them for an answer until the following day. While only mildly frustrating, it did impact productivity.

A local web designer can more easily be held accountable. If work is not delivered to your satisfaction, and the web designer is not geographically close, you may have a challenge chasing him or her down for resolution. When the person chasing you is thousands of miles away, there's very little risk that he or she will pursue you to your home turf.

There's even a corollary for web designers: a local client can be held accountable if they do not pay their bills. It does not happen often, but when I have to chase clients for payment, it certainly helps when I am physically able to confront them. In addition, since we generally know people in common, I have the leverage of embarrassing them in front of other clients or friends. While I really don't want to resort to such tactics, it does give me the leverage needed. Local reputation can be a powerful motivator for some people who might otherwise not care that a client is unhappy.

I've been approached more than once by organizations that hired a web designer long-distance, paid in advance, and then could not force delivery of their website. One of the most extreme examples was a woman in California who hired a web designer in Canada. His website gave a decent impression, the package sounded reasonable, and his work samples were good. However, after she paid in advance, he delivered a half-completed website and left her hanging for months. No amount of communication or patience on her part produced a completed product. After each reminder about the project, he'd respond by e-mail that the work was in progress.

Eventually she gave up, hired me, and we created her website. She requested a refund, which he eventually agreed to, but the check never arrived. With every e-mail, his response was that payment was coming. At this writing, it's been over eighteen months, but no check has arrived. Had she been working with someone local, she had options for small claims court and at the very least could have walked into his office to confront him personally.

Evaluating and Approaching Web Designers

In addition to technical skill requirements, your personal working relationship criteria need to be met

As well as identifying a web designer who creates work that appeals to you, you need to find a qualified web designer that meets your personal criteria of budget, timeline, personality, and working style.

Do you like to meet face-to-face? Can you rely on someone who you will only communicate with via e-mail and phone? If you want to meet the web designer who will be working on your website, then you must limit your search to people physically located within a very close distance. If you can be comfortable with communication based only on e-mail, phone, and video chat, then you have more flexibility.

Don't underestimate the importance of personality fit with your web designer

You're going to work closely with your web designer. If you have issues with his or her communication style, sense of humor, voicing of political opinions, or any other interaction, it may become a challenge to work together.

I've certainly worked with clients whose political views were different than mine. However, I'm careful to never voice my opinion in certain areas without already knowing the client's opinion on the topic—and his or her opinion about differing views on the topic! I have some local clients whose political views are very different from mine. I have occasion to encounter these clients at social and community events. While we each know which side of the aisle the other stands on, we are good-natured in our agreement to avoid political discussion. Depending on the style and duration of our relationship, we can have an implicit agreement to disagree on certain topics and still maintain great communication when it comes to my work on the website.

A former client was in another state—despite my encouragement that he find someone closer, he had seen my work and insisted that I was the right one for him. After we started working together, he frequently made caustic comments regarding the actions and opinions of the current president. I happened to agree with some of his opinions, but his behavior became so negative and destructive, I eventually had to release him as a client. His propensity to send inflammatory (and often lengthy) commentary was a distraction to my productivity.

Web designers have their own considerations and criteria in determining whether you are the right client for them

Experienced web designers have factors they consider when evaluating potential clients. Sometimes a single factor can be enough for a web designer to reject you as a client. You won't know the factors ahead of time, as each web designer has his or her own criteria.

Most web designers won't specify these constraints on their websites, so you need to ask. For example, they may prefer to work only with local clients or clients located in the same time zone. Some do not take on maintenance work for websites they did not design or create. Some do not take on work for certain types of organizations. Some are unwilling to work on websites using specific techniques or implementation methodologies.

A web designer that is desperate for work will take any clients that come along. However, if this designer is capable, qualified, and in demand, he or she can afford to be choosy. And if the designer has the option of choosing which clients to take, he or she will use it.

Web designers may ask any of these questions when evaluating potential clients:

- Is this client physically located in my geographic area?
- Does this client offer a product or service that I believe is of value and is offered ethically?
- Does this client share a customer base with any of my business partners?
- Do I have the potential need to use this organization's services, shop at its store, attend their events?
- Would I recommend this organization to friends, family, or business associates?
- Will this client recommend me to their friends, family, or business associates?
- Do we have personal or business connections in common that might be mutually beneficial?
- Do we have connections in common that will improve this person's loyalty to me and to my business?
- What is the likely demand of maintenance work for this client?
- Will this client have billable work for me other than website design, such as social media, e-newsletter, or print collateral?
- Are there any conflicts of interest? Are any of my current clients direct competitors of this new client?
- Does this client have a local reputation of being difficult to work with?
- Do I feel that this client has the financial means to pay for my services?

- If it's a new organization, do I think it has a solid business plan and a clear path to income?

- Does this client have unrealistic expectations of project budget or timeline?

- Does this client seem impatient or narcissistic?

- Is this client affiliated with any organization or political party that may reflect negatively on me or would cause others to make assumptions about my own affiliations?

Candidate Evaluation Process Overview

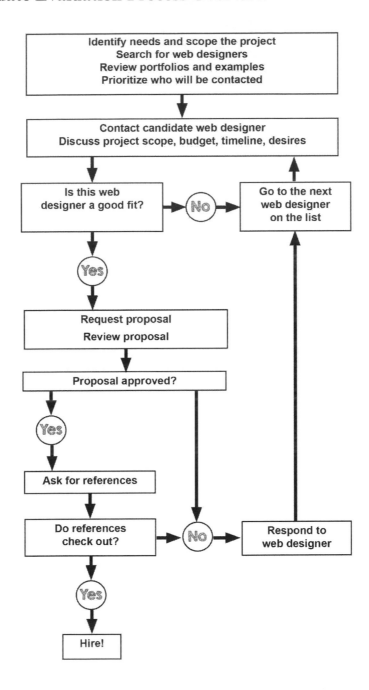

Expect and demand high quality from the person who will have your reputation in his or her hands

Review the web designer's website to assess his or her attention to detail. Look for the following issues, indicating a lack of attention to detail:

- spelling, grammar, or punctuation errors

- broken links

- empty pages

- pages labeled "coming soon" or "under construction"

- formatting issues (alignment issues, inconsistent use of fonts, sub-titles, bold, italics, text justification)

- an outdated copyright date

If you see a number of errors on the web designer's website, why would you expect that person to provide higher quality on *your* website?

I'm occasionally contacted by freelance web designers who are looking for more work, hoping that I have projects I can refer to them. While I am not looking for additional web designers as resources, I usually take the time to review their websites and provide feedback. Just by following the checklists and advice in this book, I can usually identify numerous issues and red flags quickly.

Analyze the list of past and current clients to confirm a good fit for your project

Experience with clients in your market space (or a similar one) is a plus, but don't look too narrowly. If you're looking for a web designer for your medical practice, someone with experience designing any kind of medical website will be familiar with your needs. Or if you're a nonprofit organization, a web designer who has worked with other nonprofit organizations will understand your objectives.

However, if you manage an accounting firm, and all of a candidate web designer's clients are dental practices, even a large portfolio may not be an indicator that he or she can do a great job for a business like yours.

Look for your own reflection in the client list. If this web designer has other clients with similar businesses or similar types of businesses, it means he or she has some experience with the same issues your website will have. Look for the following signs that this web designer may be a good fit for you:

- other clients in your same market space

- other clients who are your competitors

- other clients who are your business partners

- specialization in a narrow market segment

Review personal information to get the complete background and full story

In addition to looking at a web designer's work, you want to know more about his or her background, training, experience, and possibly even his or her path from a previous career to a career in web design. Look for the following items to gather more information about this web designer's history:

- information about the web designer's background, education, and experience

- an indication of why he or she pursued a career in web design

- how long he or she has been in the web design business or related fields

- ambiguous use of *we* when the organization appears to be only one person (this could indicate that there is only one person on staff, trying to appear as a larger organization)

126

If you don't see enough information to piece together these basics, you have to wonder whether the person is being careless or intentionally hiding his or her lack of experience.

Visit real websites to confirm the portfolio of sample work

Confirm that you can click through to the listed websites and prove that they are real, active websites. Don't rely only on the pictures or screenshots on the web designer's website, even with a note saying that this website is no longer active. The portfolio may show pictures of websites that are no longer available because they were later replaced by the work of other web designers. Without a link to the website, it's difficult to confirm whether this web designer actually designed it. Screenshots can be helpful but can also be created in Photoshop or grabbed from any other website.

Look for the design credit to substantiate this web designer's work

A design credit usually appears in the footer of the website. If there is no design credit on work this web designer claims to have created, ask how the work can be verified as his or hers.

Some clients feel that attributing the website to an external contractor implies being a small organization. If so, there are alternate ways for the web designer to substantiate design work:

- Include a comment in the programming of the website, which is visible by looking at the source code via the browser.

- List the web designer on the organization's staff or team page. Some clients prefer to list the web designer as a member of their staff, rather than display a design credit that shows someone outside of the organization was hired to create the website.

Exercise: Review candidate web designer website

The website includes these positive items:

- ☐ contact information, including phone and e-mail address

- ☐ name and biography for the web designer (or team of web designers), including background, education, experience

- ☐ history of how long this web designer (or web design company) has been in business or has had relevant experience in other businesses or fields

- ☐ a detailed list of services provided

- ☐ a portfolio of past work, including links to working websites

- ☐ a list of current and former clients

- ☐ information about the web designer's process

- ☐ current copyright date

- ☐ a list of frequently asked questions (FAQs)

The website includes these negative items:

- ☐ errors in spelling, grammar, or punctuation

- ☐ broken links

- ☐ empty pages

□ pages labeled "coming soon" or "under construction"

□ formatting issues

□ copyright date older than the current year

□ no names of designer(s)

First impressions count, Part I: Start with a complete introductory message to candidate web designers

When contacting a candidate web designer by e-mail, I recommend including the following information. This allows the web designer to provide a more complete response and may give him or her enough information to respond immediately in the case that your project is not a good fit.

- *Introduction:* Brief introduction to you and your organization and where you are physically located

- *Website objectives:* Is this for development of a new website, maintenance of an existing website, an upgrade to an existing website, or a complete redesign?

- *Current website status:* A link to your current website and the name of the hosting company, if known.

- *Current web designer status:* If you are looking for a replacement web designer, explain why your previous resource is no longer available.

- *How this web designer became a candidate:* Mention a referral source, advertisement, or design credit that helped you find this web designer.

- *Timeline:* Timeline or constraints for launch or implementation, external events driving the timeline.

- *Budget*: Estimated budget or financial constraints.

- *Contact information:* E-mail address, phone number, and the best method and time to contact you.

A nondisclosure agreement (NDA) may be required in order to approach a web designer to discuss the possibility of working on a project. For many projects, a conversation can be held using general terms.

However, if it's necessary to discuss proprietary information before the candidate web designer can provide a proposal, you may need to obtain a signed NDA. Your organization's legal counsel should confirm this need before you speak with candidates about designing your website.

Even if not required for an initial discussion, it may be a condition of being hired for the project or may be required before discussing the specifics of products or services.

If you do ask your web designer to sign an NDA, it needs to be specific about which tangible or significant information is covered. Unless it is specific about coverage, some web designers will not be willing to sign it.

Sample Introduction Letter #1: Business

[Replace items in brackets]

Dear Lisa,
I am the office manager of an orthopedic surgery practice in San Francisco. Our current website is [www.websitename.com] and is hosted at [name of hosting provider]. We are interested in redesigning our current website, and our original web designer is no longer in business. In addition to some new content, we would like our new website to be mobile-responsive and want to add a blog.

I was referred to you by [referring name] at [company], and she spoke highly of your work.

We would like to launch our new website no later than [date], as one of our doctors will be speaking at a conference two weeks after that date.

We are hoping that the project can be completed for no more than [$xxxxx]. After we speak, if you feel that this is not enough to accomplish our objectives, I would be happy to hear your suggestions about how we might compromise or scale back on the scope of what is needed to "go live" with the website by [date].

If you feel that this project may be a good fit for you, please contact me during business hours (Monday–Friday, 9:00–5:00) to discuss next steps.

Sincerely,

Name

Phone

E-mail

Sample Introduction Letter #2: Nonprofit

[Replace items in brackets]

Dear Lisa,
I am the development director for [organization name], a local nonprofit organization in San Jose that works with breast cancer survivors.

I found your design credit on the website for [organization name], which also works with breast cancer patients.

Based on a number of samples in your online portfolio, I see that you understand website needs for nonprofit organizations, which we feel is a plus.

We recently received a grant from a local foundation, allocating funds in our budget for creation of a website. The grant stipulates that the money must be spent before the end of our fiscal year, which is on [date].

The grant also requires that we receive at least three bids on the project. I would like to discuss our objectives and provide the RFP (request for proposal). Please contact me if you are interested in discussing this project. I am in the office Monday–Thursday, 8:00 a.m.–1:00 p.m.

Sincerely,

Name

Phone

E-mail

First impressions count, Part II: The initial response to your inquiry tells whether you're dealing with a pro

A pro will respond quickly to your initial inquiry. If you send an initial request to a web designer and don't hear back in one or two business days, it could be an indication that he or she will not respond to client e-mails quickly.

This is your first test of his or her responsiveness. If you don't receive a response within three business days, send a follow-up message or call—it's possible the original message went into junk mail. After two attempts, if you don't receive a response, you can cross this candidate web designer off of your list.

A pro will respond politely, in a professional manner, and with relevant content. The response will include a thank you for your inquiry, complete contact information, a reference to his or her website, a suggestion of next steps (such as setting up a phone conversation or meeting), and an indication of his or her availability. The designer may have additional questions of a prescreening nature, regarding your timeline, location, budget, and other factors that may determine whether he or she is even a candidate for the project.

A pro will not respond immediately with a cost or schedule quote. To give an accurate quote or to write a proposal, a web designer will need to speak with you directly or see a detailed RFP (request for proposal) document. Expect to spend thirty to sixty minutes in an initial phone conversation or informal meeting to let the candidate web designer gather the necessary information to develop a complete proposal.

Some web designers also ask prospective clients to complete a questionnaire or online form. They may even want this information before they are willing to speak with you. Many web designers want to have specific facts in hand before having a conversation or providing a quote.

Interviews

Take the time to conduct thorough interviews to confirm a good fit—no exceptions

While a face-to-face meeting may not be possible, an initial phone meeting is a requirement. You need to spend time talking to this candidate to evaluate communication and interpersonal skills.

Assess if this candidate web designer is:

- a good listener

- asking thoughtful and relevant questions

- preoccupied during the discussion

- communicating clearly

- constantly interrupting or talking over you

- explaining technical information in a way you can understand

Communication skills are a critical factor in project success

Most of what the web designer communicates or explains to you will be by phone or e-mail. If he or she can't communicate clearly, in a way you understand, that's a deal breaker.

If the candidate web designer has a heavy accent or limited capabilities in your language, that may also present challenges when it comes to communication. In an introductory phone conversation, if you can't understand what the person is saying or feel that you have to constantly ask for repetition, that's only going to lead to frustration later on.

Trust your gut: you can expect to work closely with your web designer for an extended period of time

You will need to trust this person with your online presence and with your public presentation. You must have a good feeling about this person, his or her ethics, responsiveness, and ability to engage in debate, especially when you may not agree on everything being discussed.

Then again, you may not have a specific reason, but you might get a bad vibe when you meet someone. Scientific or not, it's a valid reason to reject a candidate. I've been on the receiving end of this situation—and while it's not something that made me feel good (in the moment), it did get me out of a situation where it might have gone bad later.

A woman contacted me by e-mail, saying she had been referred to me. Following a quick exchange of basic facts through a few messages, it sounded like a good fit, and we set up a phone meeting for the next day. After just a few minutes on the phone, she abruptly ended the conversation with, "This isn't going to work. You have a bad aura, and I can't work with you." I was perplexed, but once that opinion was voiced, nothing I might have said would have changed her mind. That night at dinner with my family, we laughed about it and concluded that it was better to fail early in that type of situation. Otherwise, we might have struggled through the conversation, I would have put the time into writing a proposal, and then she would still have rejected me.

Recognize the red flags indicating that this is not the web designer you are looking for

There are a number of warning signs to indicate that this may not be the web designer you are looking for:

- a delayed response time to your inquiries or e-mails, with no logical explanation

- a refusal to accommodate an interview (either in person or by phone)

- a refusal to write a detailed proposal

- a flat per-page billing rate (all pages are not created equal!)

- a flat per-website billing rate or packages with a set number of pages

- no links to active (live website) examples of work

- example websites without a design credit or other way to substantiate the web designer's work

- poor communication skills in e-mail or an interview

Checklist: Questions for candidate web designers

- ☐ How long have you been in the web design business, and how did you get into it?

- ☐ What did you do before you were a web designer?

- ☐ What type of training or education do you have?

- ☐ Do you have a business license?

- ☐ Are you a member of the local chamber of commerce or other professional organizations?

- ☐ Can you provide links to websites you have designed?

- ☐ Can you provide references?

- ☐ How is ongoing maintenance handled for your clients? What is the expected turnaround time for typical maintenance requests?

- ☐ Do you have a backup resource to handle requests if you're not available for an extended period of time?

- ☐ Will you tell me if you're going on vacation or will be out of the office for an extended period of time?

- ☐ Are there cases where you charge extra, such as for emergencies or night and weekend requests?

- ☐ Which tasks do you partner with others to accomplish?

- ☐ What is your favorite part of the web design process?

☐ Are there aspects of the web design process that you do not handle?

☐ Are there parts of the web design process that you will subcontract to others for completion?

☐ Are there features or technologies that you specifically do not implement?

☐ Do you have any criteria you use in accepting clients?

Proposals and References

Don't hire based on a verbal quote: insist on a written proposal

A verbal quote is not documented or enforceable. If the web designer provides a price quote in a conversation (whether in person or by phone), request a written document to confirm the price quote, including the date the price was offered, any limitations on how long the offer will remain valid, and any other constraints. A price quote must also include the terms of payment.

An accurate quote is not possible without a proposal. The process of articulating the specific project deliverables and timeline will uncover details, additional costs, time constraints, and questions. Never accept a price quote that does not have the documented information to back up how that price was determined.

A proposal becomes the framework for further discussion. The proposal is essentially the blueprint for the project, providing specifications of what you are working together to create and build. This includes details of pricing, timeline, deliverables, priorities, payment, responsibilities of both the web designer and client, and completion criteria.

Candidate designers should be able to produce a proposal in a few days. A professional web designer will have a proposal template and will already know what belongs in a proposal. While writing the details of the proposal may only take a short time (I can typically do it in an hour, starting with my template), some web designers may want to do additional research before making a commitment. They may need time to thoroughly evaluate your current website (in the case of a redesign) or may want to research the websites of your direct competitors to make sure no features or type of information are overlooked.

Checklist: Evaluating proposals

Business status

Is the web designer a sole proprietor, LLC or incorporated business? Will you need to submit a form 1099 to document your payment to him or her?

Invoicing policy

Will each invoice document completed tasks being billed? What is the scope of the invoice contents? Will it list line items and deliverables? Will it list the specific time spent on each task? How are invoices submitted to you? By e-mail or paper? Are they sent on the same date each month or at key milestones in the development process? Insist on an invoice that specifies what work was accomplished or delivered. An invoice listing only total hours gives no visibility into how much time was actually spent per task. In addition, you will want a log, ordered by date, of when changes were made. If you ask the web designer to make a change on the website, you want documentation as to when that change was made. Even a simple five-minute change should be recorded so that you can trace it in history, as necessary.

Payment policy

Does the web designer require a deposit before starting work? Is payment accepted by cash, check, credit card, PayPal, online banking, or other online systems? How soon after invoice receipt are you expected to submit payment? Will you be charged a late fee or interest on overdue payments? Since your web designer has the passwords and control over the website, nonpayment may result in your website being removed from the server or somehow locked out.

Cost breakdown for the web designer's time

The web designer should be able to estimate the number of hours required for the project and assign a cost-per-hour value. It's fine if this is a range—you're just looking for validation that the web designer has actually determined the effort required to complete the project.

Costs or items billed separately from the web designer's time

Any costs that are not directly associated with the development of the website need to be listed, with details about who pays for which items. These costs could include fees for related services, such as hosting, domain registration, stock artwork, e-commerce, social media channel setup, or an e-mail newsletter.

Timeline

The timeline should include estimates for actual worked hours, elapsed calendar time, and the commitment of a start date. Some web designers will not commit to a firm completion date, because so much of the completion timeline depends on the client providing information and approvals.

Tasks and deliverables

The web designer must be able to substantiate the quoted price. Some web designers work from a page count, and others estimate time per task and add it up. Some have packages for a certain fee. Any method may be acceptable. The key is whether the web designer has put adequate time into understanding what the client wants and needs and has created the estimate accordingly.

Items required by the web designer

No matter which web designer you choose, you will be given a list of items he or she needs from each client—including technical items such as log-in credentials and content (both text and images) and "soft" information regarding the purpose of the website, the messaging, and the activities around promoting the website.

Content development

The proposal should include an explanation of content that the web designer will create, as well as the content you will be expected to provide. In the case of text, it's a reasonable assumption that all text should be original or reused with express permission of the author or owner of that text. Photos may be either those taken or provided by the client or purchased through stock imagery sources, such as online libraries.

You don't need to accept the proposal "as is"

It may be difficult for the web designer to capture all of your requirements from the initial conversation. Perhaps you forgot to mention a key fact or the web designer forgot to ask an important question. If you have concerns, questions, or feel that some elements were not covered or included, you are justified in asking for a revised proposal.

If you feel that the proposal includes items or features you don't need, ask for clarification and possible revision, especially if removing them might lower the cost of the project.

The proposal becomes the agreed upon scope of work, so you want to be sure it covers all aspects of your project as completely as possible.

Sample e-mail asking for more information

Dear Lisa,
Thank you for providing the proposal for development of our website. We have several questions that we would like to address with you. Let me know if you are willing to meet and discuss our concerns, then possibly revise and resubmit the proposal.

Regards,
Name

Take the time to respond to each proposal, even with a rejection

If you're not going to choose this web designer, take a few minutes to respond, even with just a quick e-mail message. This lets the web designer know that you have chosen another solution, and he or she doesn't need to be wondering if you received the proposal or are still making a decision.

If you have criteria that were used to select another web designer, you can include that. Even a simple message that you chose a less expensive proposal or web designer or decided to put the project on hold will be helpful (and polite).

Sample rejection e-mail

Dear Lisa,
Thank you for providing the proposal for development of our website. We have reviewed several proposals and have selected someone else for this project. We appreciate your willingness to discuss the project and provide the proposal.

Regards,
Name

Before you make a commitment, ask for several references from satisfied clients

In many situations, job candidates are interviewed, and then offers are considered, contingent on checking references. If references are to be contacted, it's usually after the interview but before the offer is presented to the candidate. It's one final check before putting the offer on the table.

While you can review a web designer's portfolio online, you will also want references around the process of working with him or her. Is the web designer prompt, responsive, courteous, willing to discuss issues, honest, collaborative, and available? You want to speak to others who have worked with this person.

Sample e-mail requesting reference information

Dear Lisa,
Thank you for providing the proposal for development of our website. We have reviewed it, and we're ready to move forward. At this time, we'd like to speak with references who have worked with you. Please provide names and contact information for two or three references.

Regards,
Name

You are free to find references on your own, without directly asking the web designer

You should be able to find work credited to this web designer somewhere on the Internet. You can look at websites in his or her portfolio and contact the organization directly.

If you find a website you like, you can always contact the owner and ask who designed it. If a design credit is available, you can click on the link. If you contact an owner, you can ask his or her opinion about the web designer, but don't just ask about design or programming skills. Is this person prompt? Courteous? Reliable? Willing to explain options and alternatives, rather than just doing whatever the owner asks (which may not always be the best option)?

I actually received a call once from someone who was checking references about another web designer. In a bizarre display of chutzpah, he had given her several example websites, claiming he had designed them. Out of a list of eight websites, several were my work and even had my design credit in the footer. In her investigation of the websites he showed her, she clicked through on footer links to find the real web designer. Once she contacted me, I did a bit of snooping around. She had originally found this web designer on

Craigslist, and through an e-mail conversation, he had responded with the list of sample work. I used another e-mail address (not my business e-mail) to contact him, pretended I was looking for a web designer, and gave him some basic specs. Sure enough, his response was a word-for-word copy of the one sent to the original client inquiry, including links to my own work. I had fun leading him down a path of conversation where I was eventually able to confront him with the false claims to my work.

The key connection was that he did design a much earlier version of one of my current client's websites. So although he had not been maintaining that website for several years, he was giving potential clients the domain name and saying he had designed it. He felt that having once designed a former website associated with the domain, he could claim he had designed the current website.

In further investigating the other websites he had claimed to design, it was the same situation, many times over. He had at one time created websites at those domains, but all had been replaced with more recent, more professional work.

Checklist: Questions for references

☐ How did you find this web designer?

☐ How long have you been working with this web designer?

Does this web designer:

☐ have fair pricing?

☐ respond promptly to e-mail and phone messages?

☐ provide detailed invoices at the task level, including time spent per task?

☐ explain alternatives and give you options in implementation?

☐ take the initiative to suggest improvements to your website or to suggest modifications from your initial request?

☐ use standard development tools (Adobe Creative Suite, or similar popular tools used by the majority of designers)?

☐ patiently explain technical issues in a way that you can understand and without excessive technical jargon?

☐ bill you for time spent on phone calls, answering e-mails, or meetings?

☐ have a backup resource when not available?

If you accept the proposal, respond to the web designer as soon as possible and schedule the project

You may need to reserve time now for work in the future, depending on the web designer's schedule, existing workload, and future work commitments.

Most professional web designers have a standard process to schedule the project and gather more information and may have additional homework assignments for the new client. If you have done the homework in previous sections, you should be well prepared for their requests.

Sample e-mail accepting proposal

Dear Lisa,
Thank you for providing the referral contact information.
You received very positive reviews and we look forward to working with you. Please let us know the next steps, in terms of scheduling our project, and what you need from us to get started.

Regards,
Name

Contracts can be valuable but are not always required

Some web designers require a signed contract from clients; some do not. The purpose of a contract is clear: it is an agreement that creates an obligation between the two parties, each of which must provide something of value to the other. The web designer is providing a website; the client is providing financial compensation for that website.

It is not absolutely necessary to have a *written* contract, as an oral contract may be legally binding in some situations. Some web designers will consider the proposal to be the offered contract.

Acceptance of that proposal constitutes agreement. If something is written down (whether a document, an e-mail, or a scribble on the back of a cocktail napkin), it relieves both parties from remembering everything discussed during the negotiation process. For projects that may span weeks, months, or years, having that record is an excellent reference point for later conversations.

Contracts can be changed after the project has started if both parties agree. It's not uncommon for the scope of the project to change, necessitating changes in deliverables, time, or cost. For most changes after the project has started, an e-mail provides the documentation in lieu of a contract.

If you pay in advance and do not receive the promised results, the contract can be beneficial in pursuing legal action. If you are not paying until project completion, you have no financial risk should the website not be completed. Let's go back to the definition of both parties providing something of value to the other party. If the web designer does not provide the website, and you do not provide payment, there is no demonstrated loss, other than time delay. If you are making progress payments, commensurate with delivered work, you are at no risk.

Do you want the web designer to sign a nondisclosure agreement (NDA)? If your organization's work involves proprietary information, and if your web designer may need access to this information prior to its public announcement, an NDA could be necessary. You may need to consult your legal resource.

Should it surprise you that my favorite contract story involves a law firm client? It's also my favorite story about tracking down delayed payment, budget increases due to constantly changing scope, and what happens when the client abuses the web designer.

The initial contact from the client was in November of 2009. I wrote the proposal and delivered it within a day, then heard nothing until April of 2010. The client said they wanted to proceed and would be getting back to me with a contract of their creation. I then heard nothing again until January of 2011. At that time, my main contact informed me that she had been out on maternity leave, and no one had picked up the project. That should have been a clue to me, but we proceeded. At that time, she again said that they would be providing a contract they wanted me to sign. That contract finally arrived in my in-box of May 2011, but I refused to sign it as written. Among other issues, the contract said I would be required to deliver the finished website within six weeks. While that was ample time to create and launch a website, I refuse to commit to a delivery date when delivery depends on the actions of the client. I can't control how quickly they deliver the necessary content or answers. After much negotiation, the contract was rewritten without the enforced completion date.

Also at that time, they received the unfortunate news that my rates had increased since the time the proposal was written (as this was now eighteen months later). Normally, when a price is quoted in a proposal, it's good for anywhere from thirty to ninety days. After that, any price increases are the responsibility of the client.

After the contract was signed, I heard nothing again until October of 2011, when I was provided with most of what I needed to complete the project. During the last two weeks of October, I did as much work as was possible, then sent a list of questions and needed items. Also at that time, I submitted an invoice on November 1, 2011, for work done to that point (as per my proposal, I bill on the first of the month for work completed during the previous month). I heard nothing through January of 2012. No check. No e-mail. No phone call. Despite repeated attempts to contact them, I heard nothing. Of course in this type of situation, I don't worry—no payment, no website. I won't get the money I deserve, but at least they won't have the product. I simply said I would not proceed until I'd been paid. Finally in April I received payment for the work done to date. I then waited for several more months before receiving the information I needed to complete the project. I took the project to the point just shy of launch and then waited another few months until the next invoice was paid.

Eventually I put my foot down and said that I would have to receive the final payment in advance of launch, given their track record. It is the only time in over fifteen years I have done this, but I did not trust them to pay me after launch. Once the website launch was complete, I handed over the login and password information and politely excused myself from any further work to maintain the website.

In Summary

Finding Qualified Web Designers

- You don't need to hire the first web designer you find.

- The best way to find a web designer is a recommendation from someone you trust.

- Find referrals through your local networking, business, or professional groups.

- Look for the design credit as a referral source.

- Hire a local web designer when possible.

Evaluating and Approaching Web Designers

- In addition to technical skill requirements, your personal working relationship criteria need to be met.

- Don't underestimate the importance of personality fit with your web designer.

- Web designers have their own considerations and criteria in determining whether you are the right client for them.

- Expect and demand high quality from the person who will have your reputation in his or her hands.

- Analyze the list of past and current clients to confirm a good fit for your project.

- Review personal information to get the complete background and full story.

- Visit real websites to confirm the portfolio of sample work.

- Look for the design credit to substantiate this web designer's work.

- First impressions count, Part I: Start with a complete introductory message to candidate web designers.

- First impressions count, Part II: The initial response to your inquiry tells whether you're dealing with a pro.

Interviews

- Take the time to conduct thorough interviews to confirm a good fit—no exceptions.

- Communication skills are a critical factor in project success.

- Trust your gut: you can expect to work closely with your web designer for an extended period of time.

- Recognize the red flags indicating that this is not the web designer you are looking for.

Proposals and References

- Don't hire based on a verbal quote: Insist on a written proposal.

- You don't need to accept the proposal "as is."

- Take the time to respond to each proposal, even with a rejection.

- Before you make a commitment, ask for several references from satisfied clients.

- You are free to find references on your own, without directly asking the web designer.

- If you accept the proposal, respond to the web designer as soon as possible and schedule the project.

- Contracts can be valuable but are not always required.

PART 4
Development

Hire your web designer, and build a working relationship of open and honest communication, trust, respect, delegation, and partnership. Design and build your website, understand the creative process, and actively participate in iterative development and refinement.

What advice would you give to a friend or colleague who is considering creating a website?

"Be ready to give thorough and honest feedback once the designer gets things up and running."

"Have an open mind. Don't think there is only one way to create your ideal website. There are many ways to do it, and if you find a good designer, they will make sure the result is what you want."

"Go for the person that will say no to you and explain why, and you will ultimately get a better product."

"Be responsive. Keep up your end of the website project plan."

"Make sure you communicate frequently with your web designer."

"Invest in clear communication to fixing the problem immediately, not back and forth to repeat the same thing all the time."

"Even though things were not completely laid out on my part, easy communication from my designer made it easy to implement changes, updates, and edits."

—Survey responses

Web Designer = Business Partner

Make your web designer a partner in your success

Your web designer is there to help you with strategic planning and ideas, as well as creative execution. Build a stronger relationship by treating your web designer as a partner in your success—not just as a contracted worker—and share your successes with him or her.

You'll need to trust your web designer on many fronts, and you want this person to:

- tell you the truth

- propose the most cost-effective methods and processes to get the work done

- be honest and up front about issues or changes

Respect your web designer's time and resources

Your web designer is also responsible for making your organization successful, so make sure his or her time is available for you. Small updates can usually be completed very quickly, but larger projects may require advance scheduling of a large block of time. Give as much warning as possible when you need a project done so he or she can allocate resources and schedule time appropriately to accommodate your needs.

Expect the best from your web designer

If your web designer provides work product that you think is not "good enough," let him or her know, and specifically explain what needs attention. You're paying for this work, so don't accept anything that is not up to the requirements set forth for the task. A professional will want to keep clients happy and will go the extra mile to rework and deliver what you need.

Listen to your web designer, and take professional advice seriously

If you have followed my advice and hired a trustworthy professional with a verified track record, then you should be able to take his or her advice seriously.

If you ask a question and then choose to ignore the answer your web designer gives you, take heed. This is similar to leaving the hospital, AMA (against medical advice). If you have hired a web designer you trust, then you can bet that the answer he or she gives you is well considered and in your best interests (assuming you gave him or her all of the necessary information to make a good decision).

A former client (a financial advisor) was already on the verge of being dismissed due to his annoying habit of calling me every time he needed a change, rather than sending e-mail. One day he called and asked me to do something that I said was misleading and misrepresented his services. I explained the expectations that came from his proposed presentation and why it was not a "best practice." He seemed to agree with my suggestions for alternatives and said he would get back to me.

A month later, he came back with the same original suggestion. When I reminded him of our earlier conversation, he argued with me about the legal (and moral) implications. A financial advisor is someone that clients should be able to put their trust in—and when the advisor is willing to stoop to immoral or unethical approaches, that's my clue to make a hasty exit.

Know which items you should forward to your web designer on a routine basis

Keep your web designer informed about anything that might affect the website, either in terms of content or administration. If you are not sure whether he or she needs to know about a specific item, timeline, cost issue, or any other aspect of the project, err on the side of asking. Early in the relationship, be up front and say, "Let me know of anything you think you should be notified about." If you're not sure whether he or she wants or needs to know something, just ask. Any of the following items might be worth forwarding to your web designer:

- maintenance or update notices from the hosting company

- reminders about payments or due dates for hosting, domain registration, or other related services, especially if you are not absolutely sure that you should be paying them

- advance notice regarding newsletters, press releases, or social media updates that might affect the website

- creation or distribution of website log-in and password information to any other service providers

Occasionally clients will receive an e-mail message asking them to pay a bill or sign up for a service. They are not sure whether it is even something they should be paying. I always tell clients that if they are ever unsure, they should forward the message to me, because I can quickly determine if it's legitimate. It is much more efficient for me to answer a question than to spend time unraveling the damage done because I was not asked.

There are many companies out there who can figure out your domain registration renewal date and send you a message saying it's time to pay them. You pay, only to discover later that they are not even your registrar. Once you send them money, you have started the process of transferring your domain registration to them, even though there is no need to do so. It's nearly impossible to get a refund on that money, since they will claim you voluntarily made the payment to start the process, and if you cancel, it's your responsibility.

Similarly, notices are sent offering search engine optimization services for a fee. While there is absolutely no requirement to pay these fees, many people will assume they are required.

Err on the side of oversharing, and keep your web designer aware of organizational news that is shared internally

If your web designer is kept in the dark about upcoming changes for your organization, he or she can't be thinking of solutions for you.

It's entirely possible that your web designer should have access to information before the general public. If so, then you should have addressed a nondisclosure agreement (NDA) at the time of hiring. Press releases are an excellent example, as they may be given to a select group in order to prepare marketing materials prior to the moment of release. If the news in the release will necessitate changes on your website, your web designer needs to know about that before the release and may need time to prepare materials before the release date.

For some clients, a press release is useful information to post on their website, but the absolute timing is not critical. That is, the press release could go out in the morning and be posted on the website in the afternoon. Then again, for businesses whose releases have financial implications (such as if the business is publicly traded), it is imperative that timing is coordinated, such that any information changes in the release are correctly updated on the website at the right time.

Depending on the changes, of course the web designer may need advance notice to have time to prepare the changes. In addition, it may be necessary for the web designer to be available to post the changes on a specific day, at a specific time.

I've worked with several clients where press releases were tightly scheduled, and I was not given advance notice. Imagine my surprise to find an e-mail about a release on the morning it's already been released (I'm in California, and the releases would typically go out at 6:30 a.m. EST).

In addition to posting the release itself, there were often other changes, such as product announcements, management changes, or other material information. Without having instructions in hand ahead of the release, it was difficult to recover. Some web designers will absolutely charge extra when faced with this situation, as they have to reprioritize previously committed work.

Don't put your web designer in the position of responding to your illegal or unethical behavior

While the typical client does not request work that violates the law, there are situations where it's possible. It's not a problem to disagree with a client regarding implementation, but when the web designer tells the client something is inappropriate and the warning is ignored, the designer may consider exiting the project.

Examples of unethical or illegal requests of your web designer:

- use of material known to be copyrighted

- use of material that is known to be false or a misrepresentation of the client's organization

- use of photos that the client does not have permission to use or photos of individuals who have not given permission to use them

- use of material that is racist, inflammatory, or libelous

- collection of e-mail addresses or personal information for the purpose of sending unsolicited messages or selling the information

- capture of sensitive information on a website that is not suitably protected (for example, a form asking for credit card numbers, when the website does not have the proper security methods in place)

- offering cash payments to avoid income declarations and tax payments

- implementing some of the negative factors of SEO manipulation, such as pirated content, hidden content, or overuse of targeted keywords

Communication and Feedback

It's up to the client to make this relationship as productive as possible

To have a successful partnership, you need to agree on what works well for everyone in terms of communication style and format, as well as expectations.

However, it will usually be the client who needs to conform with the web designer's preferences. A professional web designer has already established policies and processes that enable him or her to work as efficiently and productively as possible. In addition, the web designer can only be as efficient as the client allows him or her to be.

You can't go wrong if you are overly explicit in whatever requests you send by e-mail. I'd much prefer it if clients err on the side of explaining too much and leaving nothing to chance. Otherwise, I will need to ask for clarification or make an assumption and make a mistake—and mistakes mean rework, which can be a time-wasting *and* cost-increasing exercise.

Identify a single point of contact in your organization for communication with the web designer

Multiple sources of input lead to confusion or contradiction. If your organization has several people involved with writing or gathering content, designate one person as the primary contact, and have all information channel through that person. It's usually more efficient if the web designer is only dealing with one person when it comes to receiving input, getting instructions on prioritization, sending information back, and asking questions. Otherwise, it's possible that contradicting instructions will come in from multiple sources, and it can be difficult (or impossible) for the web designer to know whose opinion ranks highest.

I made the decision to drop a local nonprofit client whose website I was maintaining as a volunteer. As much as I supported its cause, the nonprofit's inefficiency caused me to waste more time than necessary. This organization had several annual events, and each event had an organizing committee. In each case, multiple committee members would send me conflicting information. I either had to spend time asking questions about whose request overruled whose, or I did work based on one request that had to be redone shortly thereafter because another committee member jumped in with the opposite answer.

Despite my repeated requests, they were not able to consolidate and create a single point of contact. I was forced to suggest that someone else manage the website.

Leave a paper trail: communicate change requests or questions by e-mail instead of phone

Whenever possible, documenting a website change request in writing is preferable. Changes left on a voice mail message, or via text message, are at higher risk of being missed or incorrectly transcribed. In addition, instructions left via voice mail message may be disputed later. Having a clearly documented trail of requests and responses:

- avoids confusion and finger-pointing

- reduces misinterpretation

- provides a record of when the request was submitted

- guarantees a way to track requests (if necessary, the original message can be forwarded from your e-mail "sent" folder)

- enforces processing of requests in the order of receipt

While a phone call may be required for further discussion, the initial request can always be submitted by e-mail.

I've terminated several clients who repeatedly insisted on leaving change requests on voice mail and sometimes even by text message. Despite being reminded that I won't process requests that don't come in by e-mail, they continued to do so. This was so frustrating and impacted my productivity to the point that I had no choice.

In addition to the items mentioned in the bullet list above, phone calls are disruptive to productivity. No matter what your profession may be, a phone call can derail you from the work at hand, whereas e-mail can be processed and answered at a planned time. When you answer a phone call, you immediately give that interruption the highest priority, and that client may unfairly jump to the head of the line. This also reduces productivity on the project that was receiving attention prior to the phone call.

If an emergency occurs and you must leave instructions via phone or text message, be sure to include your full name and contact information. When I receive a text message that does not contain a name, the phone number alone may not be enough to confirm who is asking.

Organize feedback and requests to facilitate efficient processing: separate information into chunks, but aggregate items into numbered lists

Separate information into discrete chunks that can be completed independently. Ideally, requests are self-contained and can be addressed independently.

Separate web page contents into separate files or on separate pages of the same file. Small chunks of information are easier to deal with, finish, test, and cross off of the larger to-do list.

Aggregate requests into organized, segmented lists. If you are sending a list of changes, group them by website page or topic. Clearly identify each page by name or link. It's more efficient for the web designer if all of the programming on one page is done at the time that file is open. Otherwise, there is duplicated effort in retrieving, editing, publishing, and testing the same file multiple times.

Present information in a numbered list so that items can be easily tracked and closed. This also makes it easy to respond by e-mail, referencing just the item number.

Effective file naming is essential to avoid confusion and miscommunication

Documents with structured and well-defined names are easier to search for, identify, and retrieve. This ensures consistency and reliability and also contributes to improved productivity in communications with your web designer.

Any files sent to your web designer should be clearly named, including your organization name, the content topic, the date, and revision number. While it may be obvious to you if the file is named "home page content," your web designer is receiving many files from other clients, possibly with similar content and names. Without the client referenced in the file name, it could be very easy to misfile.

If you have your own file naming convention, share it with your web designer so you both know how to interpret file names. Most web designers receive so many files from clients that are not well named that they are used to figuring it out. However, if you have a system in place, they can learn it.

Assign file names that are unique across all of your files and will be unique when compared to files for other clients

You may have a file with the same title or purpose in multiple directories or folders on your own computer, but it's possible that your web designer will save the files in the same folder. Unique file names will prevent issues. Always include your organization name in the file name. Your designer may receive files of the same name from multiple clients.

One recommended approach is to set up a hierarchy:

- organization name

- project name

- specific content name

- date, revision, or other sequential numbering system

Let's suppose your company is the ABC Company, and you are sending several files with website content. You might use the following:

- ABC website content About v1 022314

- ABC website content Contact v1 022314

- ABC website content Services v1 022314

Subsequent versions of these files might be:

- ABC website content About v2 022614

- ABC website content Contact v2 022714

- ABC website content Services v2 022814

Now it will be clear when the second version was created, relative to the first one. One benefit of this system is in helping to organize files within a directory, as files are ordered alphabetically. For example:

- ABC website content About v1 022314

- ABC website content About v2 022614

- ABC website content Contact v1 022314

- ABC website content Contact v2 022714

- ABC website content Services v1 022314

- ABC website content Services v2 022814

Provide feedback that is immediate, relevant, and specific

As soon as you see something—*anything*—that you question, ask your web designer about it. The longer the design and implementation process goes on, the more difficult (and expensive) it may be to make changes.

Making changes late in the project can take more time, cost more money, and force rework of other completed items.

If you have a question about how or why something is implemented a certain way, ask for clarification.

Be specific when requesting any change or correction. Err on the side of giving too much information to explain your concerns. If you can reference another website with the desired implementation (or what you are looking for), do so.

Give feedback on what is working for you, as well as what is not working

Your web designer needs to know what you are pleased with, as well as what does not please you. If you don't comment on what you are satisfied with, he or she may not know if you like something or just don't care enough to comment.

Identify device and browser dependency when reporting any bugs or issues

If you have specific feedback about how something appears on your website or if it seems broken, be sure to include whether you are looking at a Mac, PC, tablet, or smartphone, which browser you are using, and the version of the browser.

Your web designer needs to be able to recreate the problem before fixing it so that he or she has a way to confirm that it's fixed afterward.

Your web designer may also ask whether you are able to duplicate the issue (or see the same result) on a different device, or on the same device using a different browser. If you think the issue may be situation-dependent, you can test on another device or browser before reporting to your web designer.

Separate content edits from design feedback

Content edits are often more objectively correct or incorrect and can easily be addressed and checked off of a list. Design work is more subjective, and while the client should expect to be happy and satisfied with the end result, it may not be a clear case of what is good or bad. In this case, feedback will often require discussion before it can be resolved or implemented.

There are often multiple solutions to achieve the same result

- Don't assume that there is only one correct answer.

- There are multiple perspectives, and the goal is to find the answer that works for the most cases.

- Your opinion as the organization owner or representative does not necessarily reflect the thinking or interpretation of website visitors.

- There is no one website or example that is liked by everyone.

- Good and bad (or right and wrong) are not the same as what you like or dislike.

- Be clear as to whether a requested change is your opinion or a factual error that needs to be addressed.

- Some formatting choices are dictated by best practices, not just arbitrary choices made by your web designer.

Don't forward feedback to your web designer without filtering it and taking into account the source

If you receive feedback on the website work in progress, don't automatically assume that it has to go to your web designer, unfiltered. If you're soliciting feedback from multiple people within your organization, you'll need to consolidate input and possibly get clarification before submitting to your web designer. Consider the following:

- Do you think this feedback is valuable and relevant?

- Do you trust this person's judgment?

- Does this person have enough background information to understand the context of what he or she is reviewing?

- Do you think he or she is being collaborative and trying to help you make the website better?

Payment

Establish an invoicing and payment process before any money changes hands

A professional web designer will include payment policy information in the original proposal. If not, you need to ask for that information before agreeing to the project.

The payment policy should clearly articulate:

- the method of payment

- the timing or frequency of payment

- how the web designer will provide documentation to substantiate the work product being invoiced

- penalties for late payment or nonpayment

Agree on how and when your web designer will be paid

Confirm whether payment will be acceptable in the form of check, online payment, or some other method. Some businesses will charge more for clients who pay by credit card or online systems that charge transactional processing fees. Web designers are no exception and would rather not pay those fees out of their earnable wage.

Some web designers will ask for a deposit. Many will insist on progress payments and will send invoices at regular intervals (or based upon the completion of specified deliverables). This method keeps the web designer from doing too much work without compensation, keeps the client accountable for ongoing investment in the project, and provides logical, time-based boundaries for reporting completed work.

If an invoice is presented after work has been completed and delivered, then you should pay it within a reasonable amount of time—usually two weeks—unless prior arrangements have been made. If your web designer will charge a late fee or interest for bills not paid promptly, make sure you know that.

Know your web designer's late payment and nonpayment policies and penalties

If you do not pay your web designer on time, you also risk having your website shut down. Your web designer has substantial power, in terms of knowing where the files are, the passwords, and how to access the web server.

In more than fifteen years of freelance work, I have only gone so far as to pull the plug on a website a handful of times. When invoices are several months overdue and the client is clearly avoiding paying me, I have no choice. Removing the files from the server can be done very quickly—often in a matter of a couple of minutes. Restoring the files does not take much longer than that, but if I get to the point where I have to do so, I will charge the client for several hours of "penalty" time to make up for my efforts in chasing them down for payment.

Know whether you will be billed for travel time, phone calls, answering e-mail, and meetings

Each web designer has a defined process for this. In general, answering phone calls and e-mail or meeting with clients (either in person or by phone) is usually assumed to be part of the project and is part of the web designer's overhead to run the business. However, if you ask the web designer to meet in person often, to travel far, or to attend regular meetings for the express purpose of working on the project, it could be considered billable time. If something can be accomplished via e-mail, that's generally more efficient than having phone conversations and is usually not considered billable time.

Confirm who pays for any items outside of the web designer's time before any work is done

If your web designer will purchase items on your behalf, confirm whether the cost of those items is included in the overall proposal cost. Some costs are minimal (for example, three to five dollars for a single photo), and many designers will not invoice those separately. On the other hand, if you ask your web designer to purchase one hundred dollars' worth of photos, it's reasonable for him or her to expect reimbursement.

If your web designer needs to purchase software, templates, themes, or fonts to complete your project, this may also be invoiced separately.

Handle domain registration and hosting accounts yourself

Some items associated with your website will be paid on a recurring basis—monthly, annually, or even for multiple years at a time. These include domain registration, hosting, membership, and other service fees. These items are integral to the functional infrastructure of your website, and you want to be sure they are in the name of your organization or a member of your organization.

Under no circumstances should these items be established in the name of your web designer. All bills and renewal notices should come to you.

Stay on top of bills, and make sure they are paid at least one month before renewal is due. In some cases, accounts are frozen to changes if you get too close to the deadline. You can renew for multiple years in a single transaction, so if you are willing to pay a bit more now to do so, that relieves you of having to deal with it for some time to come.

Don't purchase website hosting from your designer

Some web designers offer hosting as part of their service and will bill you monthly. While that may seem convenient, it's an easy (although small) source of ongoing revenue for the web designer for doing almost nothing. It's more secure to have these services in your own name and managed by a third party whose primary service is website hosting. At some point in the future, if your web designer is no longer in the picture, then you are not in danger.

In addition, no matter how tech savvy your web designer may be, if the server is in his or her office (or garage) and your designer is not available, a server error could mean that your website is unavailable until he or she fixes it. A larger hosting company with a staff available 24-7 will be able to address issues much more quickly.

Any other services related to your website should also be in your name

This includes payment systems, registration systems, e-mail newsletters, and any other service related to the website. Think of the website as one large package, and all related elements should be in the name of your organization (or a key individual within your organization).

Keep track of expiration dates and autorenewals to avoid payment issues

Many web-related services will encourage you to sign up for autorenewal or autopayment in order to guarantee no loss of service should you forget to pay a bill. This can be an excellent strategy to avoid problems, but it can also *cause* problems. For items billed monthly, it relieves you of paying the same fee often, and you'll be notified of it with every payment. So when it's time to cancel, you'll realize it, and the worst case would be that you've paid for an extra month.

For items billed every year (or at even greater intervals), autorenewal can also cause challenges. If your credit card information changes, you'll be notified when the payment processing fails—no problem there. The issue arises when you no longer need a service and forget to disable the autorenewal. That autorenewal date rolls around, and suddenly you've been charged for the next year of services without realizing it.

Keep a list of all services related to your website, with expiration dates and whether they are enabled with autorenewal. Then, should you discontinue any of those services (or move to a new service provider), you'll be reminded to disable it.

A client called me in a panic. We had moved her website to a new hosting service provider for better functionality and improved customer support. She had not cancelled the old hosting, assuming it would just expire. Despite the fact that her website was no longer hosted there, the account was still active, with autorenewal enabled. They had charged her card for renewal to cover the next year of hosting (which she would not even use).

After several hours on hold with the support department, followed by their refusal to refund the charge, she had limited options: either accept the charge, continue fighting with the hosting service, or try to dispute it through her credit card service. Perseverance paid off, and after multiple calls over a span of more than two weeks, the charge was refunded—but at the cost of many hours and unnecessary stress!

If hosting renewal fees are not paid on time, your website will be unavailable

Depending on the hosting company's policy, the files will remain on the server for some amount of time after the website is disabled, and if you pay the bills, your website will reappear. However, if you go too long without paying, the files will be completely removed from the server, and you will have to pay your web designer to restore the website from backups or possibly to rebuild it from scratch.

A medical practice called to tell me that their website was down. No big deal: this happens all the time. I confirmed with the hosting company that the hosting bill was due and that a call to them (with payment information) would fix the issue immediately. So I assumed the client was taking care of payment and did not worry about it.

Two months later, the same phone call—the bill had not been paid, so of course the website was still down! I asked whether they had received any reminder e-mails, since that's pretty typical when a bill is overdue. No messages. They were completely unaware of the status. It turned out that the domain registration and hosting were in the name of a physician no longer with the practice. So the reminders were going to him and being ignored. The solution was to contact the hosting company to pay the bills, then change the hosting account information. Unfortunately, with more than two months having elapsed, the website files had been removed from the server, and I had to restore the website from backup, so the client was billed for that time. Had they taken care of it immediately, that situation would have been avoided—not to mention over two months with no website.

If domain registration renewal fees are not paid on time, your website will be unavailable

The domain registrar will also have no qualms about shutting down your website the day the renewal bill is due. Unlike the local utilities, there may not be a grace period for late payment.

If your domain name renewal date passes, your website will become unavailable. The files will still be on the hosting server (assuming that bill is not also overdue), but website visitors will not be able to get to your website.

After the renewal date, the domain name goes into a "holding" zone for some amount of time, during which you will still be able to renew it. After that, the domain name may be released to the public and will be available for purchase by someone else.

When a domain renewal fee is not paid on time, the registrar may think there is value in advertising that the name is available—perhaps it is something that would be in demand by another competing business or organization. Of course they have only the domain name upon which to base any advertising, so they may guess based on words contained in the domain name. Once that advertising is posted, anyone may acquire the lapsed domain name.

"Help, our website has been hijacked by a porn site." My client was a local nonprofit organization providing much needed services for elderly adults in the community. Their domain name included the word "adult"—which of course has various connotations. I received a panicked call from the executive director when the website suddenly displayed a scantily clad vixen offering the domain name for sale. Clearly, the keyword "adult" had triggered an assumption that the domain would be desirable for an adult-content website. It was the weekend, and we were unable to contact the organization's bookkeeper to handle payment, so I logged into the registrar's website to pay it immediately myself in order to restore the website.

Of course not all web designers are willing to go this extra step, so it could have escalated to a much worse situation.

The web designer has the keys to the kingdom— nonpayment can result in website closure

Remember that your web designer has control over the website, so if you don't pay, he or she can very easily remove the website from the server. In addition, your web designer can change passwords and lock you (the client) out of the system entirely.

Some web designers do not bill for work until after it has been done, so the bill is due and payable upon receipt. The website has already been updated, and the client is getting the advantage of my work without paying for it.

If, after several reminders, the client has not paid overdue bills, the next step can be to simply shut down the website and change the passwords. For this reason, most web designers do not release admin log-ins and passwords until they are paid.

The actual work to shut down and restore the website is not much, but if it gets that far, it's possible you will be charged for additional time to cover the web designer's efforts to get payment.

One memorable story involved a business only about twenty miles from my home office. Despite repeated promises of "the check is in the mail," no check arrived. And then despite my repeated threats to disable the website, no check arrived. Coincidentally, the client's wife was a teacher at our local elementary school (which was how he found me in the first place). I even offered to have him send the check to school with her, for my pickup. Still, no check.

Eventually, I disabled the website and informed him that I would need a check, plus a charge to cover two hours of my time to restore the website. Not that it would take two hours, but considering the interest-free loan of hundreds of dollars for several months and my time to chase him, I felt this was justified. He labeled it as extortion—my view was only that it was a justified expense. He eventually drove to my house with the check and stood on the doorstep demanding that the website be restored immediately—but I was not about to do that without cashing the check, so he had to wait a few hours.

Immediately after depositing that check and restoring the website, I informed him that I could no longer keep his business as a client. Several months later, I received a call from a man identifying himself as the new owner of the business. It turned out that my former client had not been paying many bills, and a supplier eventually took over his company and inventory to settle a much larger outstanding debt.

The Implementation Process

Every web designer has specific processes he or she likes or wants to use, and these have been optimized for efficiency

No two web designers will use the same process, but it goes more or less as described in the list below. Note that some web designers may choose to do some steps in parallel. For example, the client can be working on content development while the design is being developed.

1. Define the project.

2. Develop the website architecture: identify the complete list of pages, organization, and navigation schemes.

3. Develop the page structure: elements of each page, what goes in the main body, sidebars, footer, header.

4. Develop website content: text, images, multimedia.

5. Design graphic user interface: layout, colors, fonts.

6. Build and test the website architecture in staging.

7. Fill in content: create, refine, edit, proofread, revise.

8. Conduct final testing: web designer testing, client testing, audience testing.

9. Receive final approval from the client.

10. Launch the website.

11. Market and advertise the website.

12. Revise and update the website as necessary.

Ask about the staging environment, and make sure you have access to it

A staging environment is used to assemble, test, and review a website before it is launched or put into production.

The staging phase is best done on hardware that duplicates the hardware used in the production environment, which means that the staging website should ideally be on the same hosting platform as your real website.

It's imperative that the complete website be tested in the staging environment before it's launched. So while your current website is live and functioning, the new or revised website is in staging, where it can be tested and changed without anyone else seeing it. Some web designers will build the early versions of a website on a different server, but that's not going to represent the real, final home of your website, so ask for staging to be on your own hosting package.

Be sure to ask your web designer how he or she will implement the staging environment and how you will have access to it. Generally, the client is given a log-in and password to see the website while it's being developed. While you don't want to hover over the shoulder of your web designer, you also don't want to wait until the last minute to see what's going on. Much better to be allowed to observe during the process so that you can offer feedback throughout.

A client hired someone to build her website, and his staging platform was a subdirectory on a completely different server. Her domain name pointed to this subdirectory, so entering it in the browser's address bar did eventually get to the work in progress—for many months, until the point that I was hired. Not only was the website partially completed, but it was not locked up in any way so search engines (and anyone else) could find the partially completed pages.

The former designer went missing, and we eventually purchased a new domain name and built a completely new website. However, the damage done from this sort of situation can take months to undo.

Even the simplest change request takes a minimum amount of time

Even the simplest change takes time for your web designer to:

- understand your request

- clarify your request

- make the change

- test that the change was implemented correctly

- respond to you that it's done

In addition, your web designer has a long list of other changes that may be ahead of your request. Even if you think a change may take only five or ten minutes, don't assume that a quick change can or should jump to the head of the line, especially if other clients are already waiting.

Whether a client asks the web designer to change one letter, one word, or an entire page, the web designer must go through the same minimum sequence of steps:

1. Make sure he or she understands what the client is asking for, and if clarification is needed, send the client an e-mail and wait for a response.

2. Open whatever design tools are used for this client's website.

3. Open the set of files for this client's website.

4. Edit the appropriate file(s) to make the requested changes.

5. Test the changes locally (viewing in the browser on the web designer's computer).

6. Iterate to fix, adjust, and fine-tune. Sometimes the web designer can't do exactly what the client requested and may have to try

alternatives. Or he or she may implement it as requested and then realize that it won't work without adjustment for web standards or other issues.

7. Open the file transfer application, and log in to connect to the server where the website is hosted.

8. Publish any changed files to the web server.

9. Test the change in a live browser.

10. Depending on the type of change, it may be necessary to retest on all browsers and mobile devices again. If it's a text edit, testing on one browser could be fine. If it's a layout change, it may require testing on multiple browsers and devices to be sure it looks good everywhere.

11. Respond to the client that the change is done.

12. Wait for feedback and confirmation that the change was implemented as requested. After the client reviews the change, he or she may ask for further modification.

Make sure that all change requests are explicit and complete

Avoid giving the web designer a reason to come back to you for clarification. Reasons why the web designer needs to go back to the client in step 1:

- missing attachment
- unclear instructions—text, placement, order
- ambiguous instructions
- a change in one place affects the website elsewhere

Confirm all changes after your web designer says he or she is done

When your web designer responds that a change has been completed, you should also go back to test and confirm that your instructions have been correctly interpreted. There may be a programming error, but it may also be that your instructions were ambiguous or incomplete in some way you did not anticipate.

Your designer may not have tested in all possible configurations of device and browser, and you may catch something he or she missed.

Change Request Process

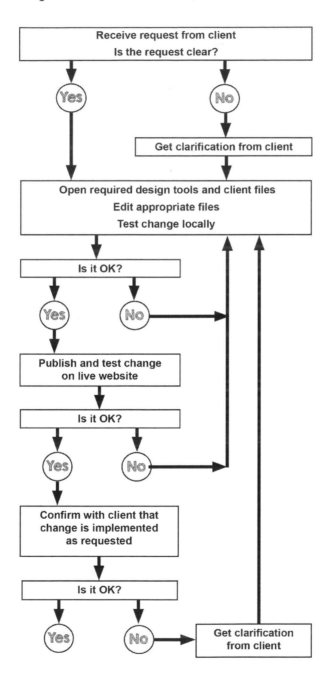

Content

Your web designer will need all of the website content, although not immediately. If the pages and architecture have been defined and blocked out, much of the work can be done before the final content is required.

Many of the items your web designer will need were covered in Part 2 of this book. So if you've already done your homework, you'll have it all ready.

Ask your web designer about preferred file formats for text

Good formats to submit content include Microsoft Word, e-mail, and PDF. However, make sure a PDF is not locked, as text can't be copied from a locked document.

Most web designers will say that text in a word processing file (such as Microsoft Word or Pages) is fine, or even plain text in an e-mail message.

Best is a separate document file that can be saved independently of an e-mail message, which may contain other information not relevant to the content.

If your text content is only available in a PDF, that's usually workable, but the web designer will have to spend more time reformatting, as it is not a simple copy and paste job, due to internal formatting in the PDF, some of which may be lost or modified as part of the copy and paste process.

Provide content by fax or scan only as a last resort

A fax or scanned document is just an image. The actual text on the page has been converted to dots for printing. If you send your web designer a faxed or scanned item, the information will need to be retyped. Before you get into that situation, confirm whether you will be charged for that time. If so, do the typing yourself, and send the finished copy to your web designer.

Have original logo artwork files and color palette information available

If someone else designed your logo, you should have a high-resolution version in your files and possibly the design source files. Although your web designer will convert your logo to a lower resolution image for website usage, it's best if he or she is able to start with a high-quality original artwork file.

If you have a defined color palette or branding standards, let your web designer know. Web designers generally work with the RGB color system. If a print designer designed your branding materials, they may be in another color system. Your web designer should be able to convert from one format to another.

Print collateral provides needed context as well as content

Files or hard copies of existing print collateral materials (including business cards, brochures, flyers, and advertisements) will be helpful. If you have electronic originals of print materials, your web designer may be able to extract text from them, so it's worth sending them. In the worst case, if content from your print collateral will be needed on the website, you can retype it yourself and send it in a document file.

Even if you're an expert on your business, you may not be an expert writer or organizer of information

You need to rely on your web designer to start with your draft work and then edit it for optimal web presentation. If your web designer is not also a proficient writer, he or she may not catch your mistakes in spelling, grammar, and punctuation and will allow them to appear on your website.

To be sure you are hiring someone who can edit your work, look at his or her website, e-mail messages, proposal, and finished work. If the writing on sample client websites is poor or sloppy, it could mean that this web designer does not edit what clients provide.

You may be an excellent writer—but not an experienced writer for the web

Text presentation on a website has its own special rules. Online readers do not read website materials in the same way they read printed materials. Web content benefits from more white space, bullet lists, line breaks, and shorter sentences.

Don't give your web designer advice about design best practices— items are formatted a certain way for a reason, such as logo or navigation placement. You might think it's interesting or unique to take a nonstandard approach in implementation, but your audience may not be willing to spend time searching for basic items, such as your contact information.

Web design is a collaborative process that requires continual feedback and iteration from both sides—the web designer and the client. As the client, you are certainly the expert on your business, but that does not mean you know how best to present it on a website. A professional web designer will listen to what you have to say and will work with you to turn it into something that is both useful and appealing to your audience. However, your web designer may say that some of your content is not usable or not the best possible way to communicate the information. Don't take it personally; he or she is not rejecting you, only your content.

Write your own original text whenever possible

It goes without saying that you don't want to directly lift text from other websites. It's copyright infringement and plagiarism. While you may get inspiration from reading another website, it's always best to write your own materials, from your perspective, leveraging your own expertise.

Some exceptions do exist: you may want to publish testimonials or endorsements as written. You may need to excerpt someone else's work as part of a review. As long as you are clearly attributing authorship in these cases, it should not be a problem.

If your organization is a vendor of a third party's product, you may have been given materials to use on your website, and this is fine. Just be sure you know the rules and assumptions defined by the vendor.

Use a spell checker on all materials you provide

It never hurts to run a spell checker on the content you send your web designer. Of course there will be multiple opportunities to proofread work on the website, but don't rely on your web designer to know the correct spelling of all technical terms related to your work. In addition, many spelling errors simply result in another valid dictionary word, so it's imperative to review for those.

Be explicit with instructions about use of technical terms

If your organization's information includes technical terms that could have multiple options or that might not be recognized by a spell checker, make sure you take the time to educate your web designer.

It happens that I have a number of clients involved with orthopedic medicine—or you may know it as *orthopaedic* medicine. Both spellings are acceptable, but each practice has chosen the one they prefer to use, and it must be consistent across all of their materials. I know to take my clues from existing client materials, but if there are ever ways to get confused, it's important to specify precisely what you prefer.

In addition, many medical or technical terms may not be familiar to your web designer. This makes the client's proofreading efforts that much more important, as the web designer may have no way to know if the words are spelled correctly.

Solicit feedback and review on your draft written materials from a knowledgeable and representative resource

Ask someone else in your organization to check your draft content for readability. If you are a solo practitioner, ask a friend, family member, business partner, or someone else you trust to do some initial proofreading.

Have a typical client check (if you have someone you can ask)—they'll be able to tell you if there are buzzwords or technical terms that the average reader won't understand.

Leave formatting of fonts and styles to your web designer

Your web designer will apply a style sheet to specify fonts, sizes, and colors of text headings, labels, and so on. Your web designer will also know more about the best formats for readability.

Use a formula or rule to order list items

If your website includes a list of items that might be updated with additions in the future, set up a formula. This makes it easier for your web designer to know where new items should be added. For example, if you list your board of directors or staff members, you should know if they are listed in alphabetical order, hierarchically by title or position, or by some other method identifying seniority.

If it is not possible to predict placement by following a formula or rule, then every time you send a new item to be added, include instructions indicating where to place the new item. For example, if you list five people with photos and bios, and you send the information for a new person, you can easily say, "Place Alice between John and Mary" or "Place Alice at the end of the list, after Jack."

If you post a list of sponsors for an event, they are usually listed in order of financial contribution, possibly in named levels (Gold sponsors, Silver sponsors, Bronze sponsors, and so on). Provide your

191

web designer with a list of sponsors, including the level and financial information, so that they can be placed in order correctly.

It often happens that existing sponsors are listed on the organization's website, but new sponsors are added after the initial list is posted. When adding new sponsors, tell your web designer specifically where the new ones go relative to the existing lineup. In addition, if you maintain a master list, you can send updated versions to your web designer so there is a way to double-check what is posted.

Try these formulas for ordering list items:

By time

- event schedule
- list of classes, workshops, or sessions

By date in chronological order

- list of classes, workshops, or sessions
- list of coming events, exhibits, programs

By date in reverse chronological order

- list of publications
- list of past events or historical timeline
- list of awarded items or recognition (such as employee of the month)

Alphabetically

- members of a team, with no implied hierarchy
- products or other items of equal value

By seniority or importance

- members of a group in a hierarchical order (such as company officers or a board of directors)
- list of awards, recognition, or memberships

Guidelines: Formatting content

Emphasis

- Use italics to show emphasis.
- Use bold only when you really need it. Overusing a bold font detracts from its ability to show emphasis. Using bold in text also detracts from the ability of headings to stand out on a page.
- Don't use all uppercase for large blocks of body text. This makes text more difficult to read.
- Don't underline text that is not a link.

Subheadings

Dividing large blocks of text with subheadings allows a reader to quickly scan content for relevance. This contributes to formatting and ease of reading.

Lists

Bulleted or numbered lists make reading and scanning a page faster and easier. In addition, bullet lists allow use of sentence fragments as a way to consolidate content where complete sentences are not required to convey a message.

Tables

Avoid use of tables for formatting unless it is the correct way to display data or results.

There is a growing focus on making websites more accessible to readers with disabilities, and tables are not easily translated for those who use screen readers on the web. In addition, tables may not translate well to mobile-responsive layouts.

If your content needs to be split into columns, you can communicate that to your web designer and let him or her figure out the right implementation and layout.

Links

Ideally, a link provides information to the reader about what will happen when the link is clicked. The goal is to use text in the link that will correctly represent what is on the target end of the link, without including unnecessary information.

If you have links to be added to your content, you can provide the information and let your web designer make the final call on the exact placement and wording of the link.

Attachment files

If your website will include attachment files for readers to download or print, there are a few additional tips:

- Give attachments explicit and trackable file names. If files will be downloaded from your website, you'll want each one to include your organization name so that website visitors will not have to guess the context should the file be in a folder with other similar documents.

- If the file has a publication date (such as a PDF version of a magazine article), include the article title, publication title, and date in the file name.

- If the file is something that may be revised in the future (such as a patient history form for a medical practice), the file name should include the date. If not, the file itself should include the date in the footer. This allows for later tracking if there is a question as to whether the person has the latest version.

Your web designer will need log-ins and passwords for a variety of items

You may balk at giving him or her this information, but if you have chosen a web designer you trust, it should not be an issue. You should always know all of your passwords and how to change them in case you need to change web designers or disable access. The web designer will give you a complete list, but for starters these include: domain registration, hosting, online payment system (such as PayPal), review systems (such as Yelp), Google Analytics, and e-mail/marketing systems (such as Constant Contact or MailChimp).

In order to obtain proprietary content, your web designer may also need log-in information for the following third-party service providers:

- ticket sales

- e-newsletters

- appointment scheduling

- patient or client portals

- social media accounts

- customer and client review websites

- job application systems

Sometimes these systems have blocks of code to be copied for embedding on your website in order to provide images, branded links, or other functionality.

Images

The visual confirmation of page content may happen with a photo or illustration, before any text has been read

On the home page, visual confirmation is especially important. Many website visitors will only stay for a few seconds, and if they do not think this website is what they are looking for, they will be gone and on to the next website.

In addition, photos and illustrations can be more interesting and visually compelling and can entice the reader to stay on the page.

Decide if you want images of people, real objects, abstract objects, or illustrations. Consistency across website images helps set the tone and provides a more consistent feel to the website.

Consistency includes:

- use of color versus black-and-white

- framing of images, including borders or shadows

- the use of images with or without backgrounds

Do not use an image from another website without permission

Doing so could be copyright infringement. If the image is a stock photo or illustration, someone has already paid for its use, so you should not expect to take advantage of that. If the image is one that was created (or paid for) by the website owner, you might be able to contact them to ask for permission to use it, but that is definitely not guaranteed.

If you use an image from another website without permission, you do so at your own risk. If you're lucky, the rightful owner of the image may just politely ask you to remove it from your website. However, stronger actions might be taken, including legal action or an invoice for inappropriate use of the image.

Requirements for file size and resolution differ between web and print

Photos straight from the camera are usually large, high-resolution images, optimized for printing. Images used on websites don't require the same resolution to display clearly on a monitor or mobile device. In addition, larger photo files take longer to load on the web page.

Image resolution is quantified in dots per inch (dpi). More dots result in more detail. A higher dpi means higher resolution. Resolution does not necessarily equate to size, but higher resolution files are usually larger, as they contain more data.

Print items generally use images of 300 dpi, although a higher dpi may be acceptable. On the other hand, web images are generally 72 dpi or 96 dpi.

If you have photos or illustrations to send to your web designer, you can always send the higher resolution files, as your web designer will know how to convert to the resolution needed.

Rename photo files before sending them to your web designer

Rename photos from the file name assigned by your camera. Many cameras use a string of letters and numbers as the file name. Sure, you can send your web designer a list of photos by number, with instructions for placement—but file names using real words will be easier to read and understand and will minimize errors when a digit is transposed.

In any case, it's a great idea to rename files so that everyone knows what is in the picture without opening the file. If the photo will be posted with a caption, you can rename the file with the caption text.

Don't send photos to your web designer directly from your phone

If you send photos from a smartphone, each photo will be labeled as *photo.jpg*, so sending multiple photos from your phone means they will all have the same file name when they land in your web designer's mailbox.

If time is not critical, it is worth the effort to send the photos from your phone to your own e-mail, save them on your computer, rename them, and then send them to your web designer. In addition, you can only send one at a time from your phone. If you save them to your computer first, you can attach multiple images to a single message.

Match up and rename pairs of before/after photos before sending

If you are sending pairs of before-and-after photos, be sure to label them so that your web designer knows they go in pairs. Many organizations are more easily advertised with a demonstration of the difference before and after their work is completed.

Usually a before-and-after picture set shows extreme change in a situation—to the point that it might not be recognizable which pairs go together out of a larger group.

A professional landscape architect once sent me a large group of before and after photos. Every "before" photo showed bare dirt or plain concrete. Every "after" photo showed lush landscaping, stonework, and new, patterned concrete. Without carefully taking the time to match up details, it was nearly impossible for me to know which "before" went with which "after" photo. I had to run through the pairs of photos with him to know which ones went together.

Similarly, when professional organizers, interior designers, painters, or tile work experts are done reworking a space, it may be very difficult to tell which photos should be paired together, because the results are so dramatically different.

Take your own photos when it's necessary

If you take photos of clients or other people who use your organization's services, you will want to get permission before posting these photos on your website. Some businesses get around that by asking friends or other staff members to pose for photos that will appear on the website. This is especially common in medical practices, where patients' privacy must be respected.

Take advantage of Creative Commons resources

Creative Commons (us.creativecommons.org) is a nonprofit organization whose express purpose is to enable sharing of materials through free legal tools. These materials may include artwork, photographs, songs, videos, and academic materials.

Their copyright licenses allow creators of work to give permission to the public to share and use that work, along with appropriate attribution. This can be a wonderful (and free) alternative to purchasing photos or artwork, and it allows the users of the work to avoid copyright infringement issues—providing they abide by the conditions specified for using the work.

There are six different license types, each of which allows a different scope of use of the licensed work. If you will be using items to which these licenses apply, you will need to understand the differences and work with your web designer to ensure that the proper attributions appear on your website.

Rely on stock images as a good trade-off in terms of time and cost

Stock images can be a great solution for many small organizations. They are easily available, well lit, and well composed, and the models have given permission for their photo to be used. To take your own photos, you will need to arrange and pay for a photographer and models (or will need to recruit volunteers), wait for processing time on the photos, and then deal with cropping or retouching. While stock photos may need to be cropped or edited for use on your website, they are also ready to use at the time you buy them.

Of course you can take your own photos, but they may not look as good. The case where you *do* want to use your own photos (or professional photos of your location), is when you want photos of your own store, office, or location, your own employees or staff, the front of your building, or before and after examples of your work.

Learn how to search for photos and illustration artwork in stock libraries

Online stock image libraries are free to search from any browser. However, most of them require membership to purchase images. They typically use a credit system where you buy a package of credits, and your account is debited with every image download. You can ask your web designer if he or she has preferred stock libraries. Ideally, you can browse and select images, give your web designer the identification number of each image, and then he or she can purchase them in the appropriate size and format.

Some web designers buy credits in bulk and will purchase images on behalf of clients, at no additional charge beyond reimbursement for the credits spent.

I prefer to purchase images myself because I will know which size and resolution is appropriate for the application. Clients may not understand this and will buy something that is either too small or too large. Since price is often scaled based on the size of the image, there is no reason to spend more than necessary.

Depending on the licensing agreement for purchased images, you may have only paid for a limited time period, which must be renewed in order to continue using the image.

Some stock libraries sell just a single license per image—allowing for only one person to have permission to use it at a time. So if you've purchased an image and fail to renew it at the expiration date, the vendor may take legal action if the image is still on your website after that date.

What? We have to pay for that image every year? This did happen to a client once, who received a "cease and desist" letter demanding payment or removal of the photo from their website, after the one-year purchase agreement had expired. The solution was to purchase a less expensive photo (which was not exclusively licensed) and change the website.

Can I use this content?

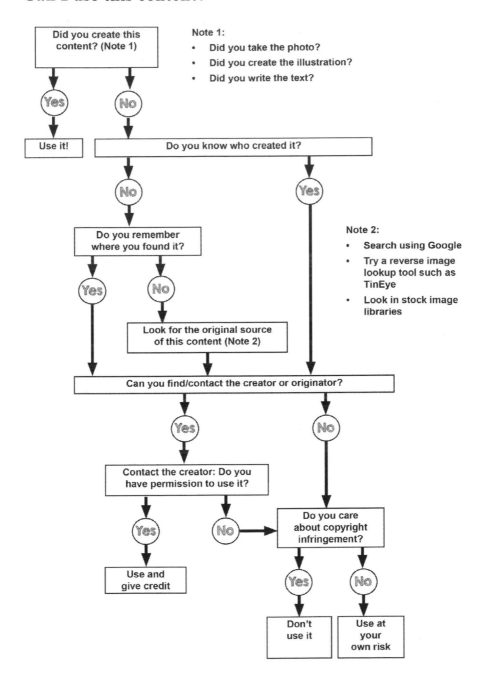

In Summary

Web Designer = Business Partner

- Make your web designer a partner in your success.

- Respect your web designer's time and resources.

- Expect the best from your web designer.

- Listen to your web designer, and take professional advice seriously.

- Know which items you should forward to your web designer on a routine basis.

- Err on the side of oversharing, and keep your web designer aware of organizational news that is shared internally.

- Don't put your web designer in the position of responding to your illegal or unethical behavior.

Communication and Feedback

- It's up to the client to make this relationship as productive as possible.

- Identify a single point of contact in your organization for communication with the web designer.

- Leave a paper trail: communicate change requests or questions by e-mail instead of phone.

- Organize feedback and requests to facilitate efficient processing: separate information into chunks, but aggregate items into numbered lists.

- Effective file naming is essential to avoid confusion and miscommunication.

- Assign file names that are unique across all of your files and will be unique when compared to files for other clients.

- Provide feedback that is immediate, relevant, and specific.

- Give feedback on what is working for you, as well as what is not working.

- Identify device and browser dependency when reporting any bugs or issues.

- Separate content edits from design feedback.

- There are often multiple solutions to achieve the same result.

- Don't forward feedback to your web designer without filtering it and taking into account the source.

Payment

- Establish an invoicing and payment process before any money changes hands.

- Agree on how and when your web designer will be paid.

- Know your web designer's late payment and nonpayment policies and penalties.

- Know whether you will be billed for travel time, phone calls, answering e-mail, and meetings.

- Confirm who pays for any items outside of the web designer's time before any work is done.

- Handle domain registration and hosting accounts yourself.

- Don't purchase website hosting from your designer.

- Any other services related to your website should also be in your name.

- Keep track of expiration dates and autorenewals to avoid payment issues.

- If hosting renewal fees are not paid on time, your website will be unavailable.

- If domain registration renewal fees are not paid on time, your website will be unavailable.

- The web designer has the keys to the kingdom—nonpayment can result in website closure.

The Implementation Process

- Every web designer has specific process he or she likes or wants to use, and these have been optimized for efficiency.

- Ask about the staging environment, and make sure you have access to it.

- Even the simplest change request takes a minimum amount of time.

- Make sure that all change requests are explicit and complete.

- Confirm all changes after your web designer says they are done.

Content

- Ask your web designer about preferred file formats for text.

- Provide content by fax, and scan only as a last resort.

- Have original logo artwork files and color palette information available.

- Print collateral provides needed context as well as content.

- Even if you're an expert on your business, you may not be an expert writer or organizer of information.

- You may be an excellent writer—but not an experienced writer for the web.

- Write your own original text whenever possible.

- Use a spell checker on all materials you provide.

- Be explicit with instructions about the use of technical terms.

- Solicit feedback and review on your draft written materials from a knowledgeable and representative resource.

- Leave the formatting of fonts and styles to your web designer.

- Use a formula or rule to order list items.

- Your web designer will need log-ins and passwords for a variety of items.

Images

- The visual confirmation of page content may happen with a photo or illustration, before any text has been read.

- Do not use an image from another website without permission.

- Requirements for file size and resolution differ between web and print.

- Rename photo files before sending them to your web designer.

- Don't send photos to your web designer directly from your phone.

- Match up and rename pairs of before-and-after photos before sending.

- Take your own photos when it's necessary.

- Take advantage of Creative Commons resources.

- Rely on stock images as a good trade-off in terms of time and cost.

- Learn how to search for photos and illustration artwork in stock libraries.

PART 5
Delivery

Launch and announce your website. Keep your website current in both content and presentation. Know the options if your web designer relationship status changes.

What do you wish you had known before working with a web designer?

"Have all your ducks in a row prior to meeting with your web designer. Getting your information to your web designer in a timely manner will start your process off on the right foot."

"An overview of the whole process with an idea of what information and content I needed to organize [and how to organize it] before I started with the web designer. I had general ideas, but once I got into it, I realized that I needed a more guided thought process to distill those ideas down before I started."

"I wish I had known that I should not trust a family member to handle such an important part of my business. Although you are not paying this person, you lose more money because the website looks cheap. He does not make changes when you need them. I would sometimes wait three months for him to change my event page. You then take things into your own hands and hire a new website designer, but now your family member is mad. I wish I had known that you should always work with a pro."

"I wish I had a better sense of what to expect as far as what I needed to produce as opposed to what the designer would produce. I also like knowing all the variety of options to me so that I can make better choices (everything from layouts available, to fonts that can be used, to special features that could be built or bought)."

—Survey responses

Launch

Launch timing is dependent not only on your organization but on your web designer's schedule

If possible, launch in the off-hours of nights or weekends. An exception would be if your current website will be replaced by a new website, and that's the exact time period where your current website is getting the most traffic. Many web designers prefer to launch websites at night or on the weekend, when they know that they will have a solid block of uninterrupted time. During the launch process, there are a number of details to attend to, in a specific order. That block of time needs to be scheduled around meetings, phone calls, or other activities.

The launch process is not just the flip of a switch: a many-step checklist must be followed

My own website launch checklist has over thirty steps, some of which are very quick (checking or unchecking a box on an admin screen), while others require more time.

Launch tasks could include:

- removing any password protection on the website that may have been in place while under development

- testing every link that goes to another page on the website

- testing every link that goes off-site

- submitting each form on the website, making sure that the form results go through to the right person and that the thank-you page is displayed after the form submission is complete

- checking all situations that result in error messages

- checking all page title tags

- testing that the 404 page (the page that is displayed if a link is connected to a nonexistent page) is working

- removing pages that were used in the old website that might still be on the server

- testing all redirects from the file or page names of the old website to the corresponding pages on the new website

- if the website includes e-commerce, confirming that purchases are placed in the cart correctly and that financial transactions are processed to completion

- running backups and confirming that backups are set to run automatically in the future

- testing on multiple browsers on Mac and PC and testing on mobile devices (including tablets and smartphones)

- checking that Google Analytics or another statistics and traffic analysis package has been installed

- confirming that blog comment moderation is working

- updating any plug-ins or additional tools, deactivating any that are not being used

- removing images or attachments that are on the server but no longer being used.

- submitting the sitemap to Google and other search engines

Your current website might be unavailable during the launch process

If you have an existing website and will be replacing it with a new one, your website might be unavailable or in a partially completed state during the launch—for a few minutes, or possibly up to a few hours, if there is a problem to resolve—so it makes sense to do this when fewer potential customers are likely to be viewing it. Depending on your organization's normal business operation, this could be at night or on the weekend.

You must be available for final testing and approval immediately after launch

Most web designers will not launch a website until the client has given approval on the final version in staging. In addition, as soon as the website has been launched, the client will—and should—be asked to review again and give final approval. Even though the web designer will be doing a lot of testing, it's always best to have a second person looking at everything again.

Ask your web designer to be available for at least two business days immediately after the launch

Some web designers will not schedule a website launch if they will not be available immediately afterward. It's possible that errors will need correction or an unanticipated issue will need immediate attention. So, for example, it would be unwise to launch a new website the day before your web designer leaves for vacation or the day before attending an all-day business conference. You want your web designer to be available and on call for immediate follow-up corrections.

Take ownership of publicizing your website after launch

You may want to send an e-mail announcement of your new website to family, friends, and current clients. You may want to announce the website on social media channels. These announcements can be prepared ahead of time so that they are ready to go as soon as you are ready to announce.

Exercise: Website publicity

To publicize our website, we will:

- ☐ add the website to all print collateral (business cards, brochures, letterhead, envelopes, flyers, newsletters, fax cover sheets, ads, stickers, and shopping bags)

- ☐ add the website to e-mail signatures

- ☐ add the website to promotional materials (key chains, coffee mugs, pens and pencils, apparel)

- ☐ announce on social media channels

- ☐ send e-mail announcements to family, friends, and clients

- ☐ send postcards to family, friends, and clients

- ☐ post signs at our office or place of business

- ☐ post the website in the window of our office or place of business

- ☐ add a decal, door magnet, or custom license plate frame to organization or personal vehicles

- ☐ place an ad in local print newspapers

- ☐ place an ad on local websites

- ☐ post an online press release

- ☐ write an article about the new website for our organization's newsletter

- ☐ mention the website when interviewed (print, TV, radio, webcast)
- ☐ include the website in promotional materials that go with prizes donated to local charities or events
- ☐ write a guest post on another organization's blog
- ☐ submit an article to a local newspaper
- ☐ submit an article to one or more websites
- ☐ add the website to the organization's listing in the local chamber of commerce or networking group directories
- ☐ add the website to listings in professional organization directories
- ☐ create a video and post on YouTube or Vimeo
- ☐ host a webinar
- ☐ publish an e-book
- ☐ blog regularly and set up an RSS feed
- ☐ publish photos on Pinterest, Instagram, G+, Picasa, Tumblr, Flickr
- ☐ create an infographic in our area of specialty

Maintenance and Beyond

Don't expect your web designer to see or respond to e-mail outside of standard business hours

For businesses that have a regular schedule of open hours (weekdays only or regular hours each day of the week), clients will only schedule appointments or walk into the store or office during regular hours. For web designers, there are no "regular" hours, as clients can send an e-mail any time of day or night, including weekends and holidays. Many web designers work very flexible hours, due to other constraints or personal preference. A request that comes in at 9:00 a.m. may be processed by 11:00 a.m., but a request that comes in at 5:00 p.m. may not be processed until 10:00 p.m. or even the next day.

It's fine to send a change request to your web designer at night or over the weekend, but it's not reasonable to expect that it will be processed before the next work day. If you send a request over the weekend and it's not urgent, include a note in the message, saying whether it can wait until Monday.

If you will need an update or change posted on Monday, send it to your web designer no later than Friday morning to ensure that he or she is aware of it and can schedule appropriately. A request that comes in on Sunday night has to compete with everything else already scheduled for Monday morning.

Some web designers charge extra for tasks that are requested urgently at night, over the weekend, or on a holiday. Like most people, your web designer would prefer to have a day off from work on major holidays.

Advance notice of several days is always best

If you know a big project is coming that will require more than ten to fifteen minutes, give your web designer advance notice. A short e-mail saying, "We'd like to publish our new schedule by May 1; will that work for you?" is extremely helpful. For a large project, ask your web designer how much lead time is required. That is, ask how far in advance he or she would like to receive the final content, relative to the requested publication date.

In general, a ten-minute task can be worked into someone's daily schedule. Most quick requests can be handled within a day or two. But if the task will take two to three hours to complete, your web designer may not have a large block of time available for it immediately.

Identify what to do with content that has an expiration date, and keep a calendar to check on it

When you send content that will expire or be out-of-date at some point, also specify on which date the item can—or should—be removed.

For example, if your store is having a sale from October 1 to 10, it needs to be removed from your website after the store closes on October 10 and before the store opens on October 11. Your web designer may figure that out when the information is first posted, but don't leave that to chance. When you send the initial request, just add, "And please remove this after close of business on October 10."

Some web designers keep a "futures" list of items that they know will have to be done at some later point in time. Keep your own "futures" list, and send a reminder to your web designer a day before the removal date

So in the above example, send a note on October 9 saying, "Just a reminder that you can take the sale off of our website after the store closes at 8:00 p.m. on October 10."

If you don't bother to do this, no harm may come of it, but having an outdated announcement on your website certainly looks unprofessional and careless.

Take advantage of multiple communication channels to let your web designer keep an eye on you

If you send a newsletter as part of your organization's communication strategy, add your web designer to your mailing list. Then he or she will always receive whatever information you are sending to clients. It's possible that you will send an announcement and forget to notify your web designer about corresponding website changes. If he or she gets the newsletter, your web designer will either know what to do with the information or will know to contact you.

Send an advance copy of all messages and newsletters to your web designer so he or she can review content and determine what must be added to your website before you send the message. He or she may bill for this time, but in the end it will save you time and money if your web designer happens to discover something that needs attention before the message is sent.

Connect with your web designer on Facebook, LinkedIn, and other social media channels. If you're lucky, your web designer may see items you post, realize that the information belongs on the website, and update without being asked.

It happens fairly often that clients make an announcement via newsletter or social media, where there is some impact on the website. If I have not been notified in advance, there's a good chance that their clients will get to the website before I have a chance to post the information. This happens frequently when a client has a new class, workshop, or event to announce. The client is so excited about sending out the announcement that he or she forgets that the website also needs a link to the registration system or may even need the registration button implemented.

Make website updates part of a regular process

If you set a regular schedule for updates to your website, your web designer will already know the work is coming and can plan accordingly to be available to meet your needs. For example, if you post a regular class schedule on the first of the month or update a calendar every Monday, your web designer will know to expect those updates. Regular updates could include calendars, coupon expiration dates, store specials, and newsletters.

Avoid sending updates on the first of the month

Depending on what is being updated, the first of the month may be a natural day for updating. However, that's true for many businesses, so your web designer could be overloaded on the first of the month. If it's a calendar for the coming month and can be posted on the twenty-fifth of the current month, that might work better for your web designer. This is the type of detail you can work out when you first create the website and then keep to the schedule.

I have many clients with updates that make sense for the first of the month, but we almost always have the information prepared early so that I can be ready for publication. Examples include:

- the weekend music performance schedule at a restaurant

- the class schedule at a knitting store

- the menu for local meal delivery to housebound seniors

- coupons for monthly specials at a dance or costume store

- special monthly class packages at a Pilates studio

Be explicit with all change requests

Any time you want to communicate a change to your web designer, run through a checklist to make sure you provide all of the information needed.

The change: Include the name of the page and explicit instructions regarding what needs to be changed, added, or deleted. If there may be ambiguity in the request, be as explicit as possible.

The type of change: This includes adding new content versus modifying existing content; adding new functionality versus modifying existing functionality; and making a cosmetic or layout change.

The priority level of the change: Is this an emergency (must be fixed immediately), something urgent (should be fixed by the next business day), or a flexible change that should be made when convenient but not on a rush basis?

If you're adding something new to a list, specify where it goes in the list, relative to existing items.

Many web designers provide online forms for clients to submit change requests—the form helps guide the client in providing the necessary information.

Exercise: Change requests

What type of change is it?

☐ add new content (new pages)

☐ modify existing content (changes to current pages)

☐ add new functionality

☐ modify existing functionality

☐ make a change to the look of the website (color, font)

☐ make a change to the layout of pages

☐ add or change a photo

☐ add or change a PDF or attachment

What is the priority level?

☐ emergency (same day)

☐ urgent (next business day)

☐ flexible

Other

☐ There is a completion deadline.

Date:

☐ We want to review the change in staging before it's published to the live website.

Just like people, websites need regular checkups

Websites don't necessarily need a checkup because they're sick, but because you want to practice preventive medicine. Your website should be checked on a regular basis so that small items can be addressed before they become big projects.

Your website will not be up-to-date without your continued effort

Doing nothing is the same as moving backward. If you don't have time to monitor your website 24-7, it's likely that some information needs to be updated, changed, or deleted. In fact, the entire website may need an overhaul.

Your competition is moving forward, even if you are not. Even if there are no problems with the website, your competitors are building and updating websites, causing you to fall behind.

Your website needs to keep up with technology changes. At the rate technology changes, new features, functionality, trends, and usability realizations show up every day. Your web designer may be making incremental changes to your website based on these changes, but unless you are specifically requesting it, that could be unlikely.

If you're considering a redesign, it's the perfect time to review and update content

Even if it's not time for a redesign, it is still worthwhile to have a content review.

Contact information

- Have any of these items changed: location, phone, fax, e-mail, hours of operation?

Staff

- Is the staff list current?
- Do bios, CVs, or photos need updating?

Resources

- Are all of the resources listed still current?
- Are new resources available to add to the list?

Check all links

- Do all off-site links still work?
- Note: link-checking tools are available to install on your website that will let you know when off-site links are no longer active

Other content that may need updating:

- photos
- descriptions of services or products
- prices
- calendar items
- coupons and expiration dates
- news coverage or mention in the paper or online articles
- giveaways or contests

Navigation and architecture

- Is your information still organized in the best possible way to reach your audience?

- Have new pages been added to the architecture one by one? It may be time to take a step back and reorganize from a fresh perspective.

Graphics

- Has your logo been changed or updated?
- Do your newer marketing materials have a different look?

Social media

- Do you now have Facebook, Twitter, LinkedIn, YouTube, or other social media channels that are not linked to your website?

Search engine results

- Is your website ranking where you want it to on search engines? Results can change based on changes in ranking algorithms and whatever your competitors may be doing to improve their own results.

Even if you were thrilled with your website when it was designed, the environment has changed

Even if the content is perfectly accurate, many other factors change over time. For most websites, a redesign or refresh every two to three years is appropriate. At the very least, a complete content reevaluation should be done that often.

New uses and objectives are discovered or invented. Brand new ways of using websites seem to appear every day. So it may be time to think about new items you can feature on your website (such as coupons, social media, and blogs). And even the way people read websites has changed, in terms of what they expect in navigation and organization.

As styles change, the look and feel of your website should be adapted

Even the increases in monitor resolution have affected web design, and mobile devices have really changed the game. Increasingly, web users are becoming more knowledgeable and know what looks like a dated design and what does not—and some people may make buying decisions based on that factor.

Technology is updated more quickly than your website

Technology on the web changes at a fast pace—sometimes it seems to be daily. New and improved ways to do what your website already does will (or have) come up. We all need to keep up with the competition and offer a good online experience. If your website is more than three or four years old, it was probably implemented on software that is no longer state-of-the-art. In addition, hosting companies change their support structures and can even decide to no longer support older implementation methods.

New browser versions—and even new browsers—are introduced and the programming of your website may no longer be compatible. Even well-designed and professionally programmed websites can experience problems in new browsers. When I create new websites, I test on all current browsers, but as the new versions come out, everything can change. If a website is a few years old and the client has not come back to me during that time for content updates, it's unlikely that I have tested it with all of the latest possibilities.

Exercise: Is it time for a redesign?

☐ Our content is no longer fresh and relevant.

☐ Our content is not updated regularly.

☐ Our website no longer represents our current mission, purpose, or values.

☐ Our website no longer presents current products and services.

☐ There are functions or features on our website that are no longer used.

☐ Our website design looks old or dated.

☐ There a number of items on our website that need fixing.

☐ A large amount of content needs to be added to our website.

☐ Website traffic is down.

☐ Our website's navigation doesn't make sense.

☐ Our website does not look good on mobile devices.

☐ Our competitors' websites look better than ours.

☐ It's been over two years since the last redesign of our website.

☐ The copyright statement on our website does not show the current year.

☐ Our target audience has changed, or a new audience has been added that is not addressed by the current implementation.

Changing Situations

Changing needs and circumstances may indicate a need to change web designers

There are a number of reasons why it may be time for a change, and you need to be prepared for this eventuality.

Something about your relationship with your web designer is no longer working

- Your web designer's behavior or working styles no longer meet your expectations.

- Your web designer is unable to provide the service you need in your desired or required time frame.

A new resource or alternative has presented itself

- You now have a member of your staff who is able to manage the website.

- Your organization has acquired a larger package of related services that includes a website.

- You now know another web designer that might be a better fit for your organization—perhaps a business partner that you are working with on other types of projects.

Your web designer's business model has changed

In that case, hopefully you will be given the courtesy of advance notice and possibly an offer of help with the transition to a new solution. It's possible your web designer might be:

- closing his or her business
- cutting back his or her client workload for personal or other reasons
- refocusing to a different client segment, and you no longer fit his or her criteria
- moving out of your geographical area

Your web designer is unhappy with you

Perhaps you are not paying your bills promptly or have gone to your web designer with too many last-minute, urgent requests. If your web designer specifies an issue that you are willing to address, you may be given another chance. If you're not willing to address the issue, it's up to you to find a replacement.

No matter who terminates the relationship, finding a new web designer is your responsibility

If you're going to part ways with your web designer, it's time to revisit Part 3 of this book.

If you part on friendly terms, your web designer may be able to refer you to someone else capable of providing the services you need.

If your web designer quits, goes out of business, or fires you, it is not his or her responsibility to find a replacement. If you're lucky, he or she might have someone to refer you to, but it's not his or her problem to solve.

Communicate clearly with your web designer about the reasons for termination

If it's time to replace your web designer, don't send notification via e-mail or text message. If you are not physically able to meet with the person, at least do it in a phone conversation. Don't leave the message on a voice mail, but leave a message that you want to speak with him or her.

- Be clear about exactly why you have made this decision. If it's due to a change in your organization or its needs, be sure to mention that clearly.

- Give specific examples of where your web designer is not meeting your expectations.

- Assuming you previously notified your web designer that expectations were not being met, remind him or her of that. Make sure to document (e-mail or otherwise) any previous warnings.

- Be clear and professional.

- Do not react emotionally to your web designer's response. When someone is let go from any type of employment, he or she may cry or argue. Stick with the facts. Allow your designer to express his or her emotions without interruption.

- Don't back down. Once you have decided to replace your web designer, don't feel obligated to give in to pleading or whining.

- If you have a contract that requires notice of termination within a time frame, be sure to honor that commitment.

Maintain control over your domain registration and hosting accounts to minimize potential problems when changing designers

When you change web designers, you need to make sure your current web designer can no longer access your accounts or files. Assuming that your current web designer has the log-in information, as long as you can change it and he or she can't access the new password, you're fine.

There are several possible situations regarding the administrative tools of your website when it's time to change web designers. In the following, "control" means that the account is in your name, you pay the bills, and you have the top-level log-in information.

Situation 1:

- You control the domain registration account.

- You control the hosting account.

Solution: Log in to the accounts, and reset all passwords. This information can then be given to your new web designer.

Situation 2:

- You control the domain registration account.

- Your current web designer controls the hosting account (he or she signed up for it in his or her name, or your web designer is also your hosting service)

Solution: If your current web designer will not cooperate, you will need to find new hosting. You will either need to duplicate your current website at new hosting or build a new website. It's possible that your new web designer can download or copy part of the existing website to the new location, but without the current web designer's cooperation, that will require some stealthy work behind his or her back.

Situation 3:

- Your current web designer controls the domain registration account.

- Your current web designer controls the hosting account.

Solution: This is the worst possible case, in that your current web designer has complete control over your website and is not required to do what you ask.

In the best outcome, your current web designer will work with you to transfer ownership of the accounts to your organization. However, you may have a challenge if he or she will not cooperate. If your web designer chooses not to transfer ownership and also chooses not to pay bills, you may be at risk of losing your website.

Your best option at that point would be to deal directly with the service providers and hope that you can clearly substantiate that the domain should belong to you. Perhaps the domain name is your actual name, you can provide proof (driver's license, passport, business documentation), and you can clearly show how the designer is a designer who registered the name on your behalf but should not be the owner. There have been successful cases of appealing to the domain registrar, but these are evaluated on a case-by-case basis and are time-consuming, and there is no guarantee.

Exercise: Is it time to change web designers?

Our web designer:

- ☐ is not responsive to e-mails and phone calls

- ☐ is not meeting time commitments

- ☐ does not have the skills to do what we need

- ☐ is no longer in business

- ☐ is changing the focus of his or her business or working only with certain client types

- ☐ has too many clients and is not providing the attention we deserve

- ☐ is making too many mistakes in implementing our requests

- ☐ is not sticking with the terms of our written contract or verbal agreement

- ☐ is overcharging or is now charging for time answering every e-mail or phone conversation

- ☐ is doing things without our permission that could reflect negatively on us, our website, or our organization

- ☐ is being rude or treating us (or others) poorly

- ☐ is overwhelming us with technical information beyond our understanding and beyond what we need

☐ is a relative or friend who is no longer meeting your needs ("Don't hire someone you can't fire")

☐ is no longer looking for *our* best solution

Our organization:

☐ now has a staff member who can manage our website

☐ has acquired a larger package of services that includes a website

☐ has identified a web design resource that is a better match for our needs

Plan ahead when it's time to shut down your website

There may come a day when you need to shut down your website. You're going out of business, or you have decided that you don't need a website anymore. Perhaps your organization has merged with another one that already has a website. Perhaps the website was intended for short-term use, such as a one-time project or event.

Let your web designer know your plans so that appropriate notices can be posted in advance and so the loose ends can be cleaned up. You will want to cancel (or choose not to renew) hosting and domain registration accounts, as well as other accounts. If any services have been set to renew or bill automatically, make sure those are turned off.

Depending on the situation, you may want to keep the website around for some time, even if the business is no longer active or the event is past. This could be for historical value and allows a smoother transitional message, rather than suddenly discovering that a website is missing.

Exercise: Shutting down your website

We need to cancel the account or turn off automatic renewal for:

- ☐ website hosting
- ☐ domain registration

We need to cancel the account or turn off automatic renewal for third-party services for:

- ☐ ticket sales
- ☐ e-newsletters
- ☐ appointment scheduling
- ☐ patient or client portals
- ☐ social media
- ☐ customer or client review systems
- ☐ job application systems
- ☐ other: _____

We need to:

- ☐ set up a redirect from the domain name to another website
- ☐ other: _____

If you buy or sell a business, the website is an important piece of marketing collateral that should be part of the overall package

The website is a valuable piece of marketing collateral for any organization. If you sell your business or transfer ownership of your organization, you'll want to specify how the website is—or is not—included in the deal. If the organization will keep the same name, and maintaining the same domain name is desirable, plan to transfer ownership of the domain registration and the hosting package, as well as any other related online items.

Related items could include other branded online systems that work independently of your website (such as social media channels) or third-party services that are directly integrated into your website, such as your newsletter sign-up, online scheduling, or payment systems.

There are a number of ways this scenario could play out. For example, the new owner may want to:

- keep the domain name and website "as is" with all related components at the same vendors

- keep the domain name and website "as is" in look and functionality but change some of the components

- keep the same domain name but build a new website at the same hosting provider

- keep the same domain name and build a new website at a different hosting provider

- keep the website but change the domain name and branding

The details will need to be worked out at the time of the change. If you are the one acquiring the website, you'll need to request all log-ins and passwords. One option is to enlist the help of the previous owner's current web designer to facilitate the transfer (and expect to pay for that person's time). Even if you have your own web designer that you would like to use, it's a good idea to engage the person who is already most familiar with the system to make the transition as smooth as possible.

If you are the one acquiring the website and want to bring your own web designer into the picture, you can ask both web designers to work together to facilitate the transfer process.

If you are the one transferring away ownership of the website, notify your current web designer and let him or her know the details. If he or she is interested in continuing to work with the new owner, you can pass along the contact information to both parties and let him or her determine the next steps.

Exercise: Changing ownership of an organization's online presence

Whether you are the current owner or the new one, confirm which of the following items are included in the transfer of a website:

- ☐ domain name registration
- ☐ hosting package
- ☐ blog (if separate from the main website)
- ☐ Google Analytics or other statistical analysis package
- ☐ electronic newsletter (such as Constant Contact or Mailchimp)
- ☐ e-commerce platform
- ☐ payment system used by clients
- ☐ online scheduling system used by clients
- ☐ e-mail addresses at the current domain
- ☐ e-mail addresses on another system (such as Gmail or e-mail associated with the Internet service provider at your organization's physical location)
- ☐ Facebook
- ☐ LinkedIn

☐ Twitter

☐ other social media platforms

☐ any special third-party specialty applications related to your organization

☐ other: _____

In Summary

Launch

- Launch timing is dependent not only on your organization but on your web designer's schedule.

- The launch process is not just the flip of a switch: a many-step checklist must be followed.

- Your current website might be unavailable during the launch process.

- You must be available for final testing and approval immediately after launch.

- Ask your web designer to be available for at least two business days immediately after the launch.

- Take ownership of publicizing your website after launch.

Maintenance and Beyond

- Don't expect your web designer to see or respond to e-mail outside of standard business hours.

- Advance notice of several days is always best.

- Identify what to do with content that has an expiration date, and keep a calendar to check on it.

- Take advantage of multiple communication channels to let your web designer keep an eye on you.

- Make website updates part of a regular process.

- Avoid sending updates on the first of the month.

- Be explicit with all change requests.

- Just like people, websites need regular checkups.

- Your website will not be up-to-date without your continued effort.

- If you're considering a redesign, it's the perfect time to review and update content.

- Even if you were thrilled with your website when it was designed, the environment has changed.

- As styles change, the look and feel of your website should be adapted.

- Technology is updated more quickly than your website.

Changing Situations

- Changing needs and circumstances may indicate a need to change web designers.

- No matter who terminates the relationship, finding a new web designer is your responsibility.

- Communicate clearly with your web designer about the reasons for termination.

- Maintain control over your domain registration and hosting accounts to minimize potential problems when changing designers.

- Plan ahead when it's time to shut down your website.

- If you buy or sell a business, the website is an important piece of marketing collateral that should be part of the overall package.

Conclusion

Maybe you read this book cover to cover in preparation for an upcoming website project. Maybe you read only one of the five parts, relevant to your current location in the website design timeline. Or maybe you scanned a few relevant sections to pick up key points that could be helpful in your present situation. In any case, I hope you discovered tips and tricks that will enable you to find and hire the right web designer for you (and for your project), or perhaps to confirm that your current web designer is the right person for the job. And if that is *not* confirmed, you now have tools to help you find your next web designer.

Most importantly, I hope my suggestions will enable you to participate as a more efficient and productive collaborator with your web designer, allowing you to work together to build the best possible website for both your short- and long-term needs.

I stated in the introduction that hiring a web designer should not be a one-time, short-term project. Your goal is to build and nurture a successful, enduring business partnership. Keep this book handy and skim through it occasionally. It's possible that your situation may change. Sections you previously considered unimportant to your situation may one day be of great relevance. Knowledge acquired over time may help you recognize value in items you skipped on first reading.

My husband is an avid and accomplished chef, with an overflowing bookshelf of cookbooks. His theory is that if a cookbook provides just *one* recipe that he can label as a "keeper"—and incorporate into his recipe box of favorites—then it was worth purchasing and keeping in his library. I hope this website cookbook has provided a keeper or two for your own recipe box.

Acknowledgments

I would like to express my appreciation to the many people who contributed to the process of writing and publishing this book.

Without the many fine (and occasionally frustrating) examples provided by clients, I would not have been inspired to document this wisdom for the benefit of others. Each client—clueless, adored, and everything in between—had something to teach me, whether technical, business, interpersonal, or project management skills. My clients have been the single most important factor in providing satisfying work that is anything but boring or commonplace.

My husband Mike patiently tolerated many years of nightly dinner table installments of client stories. He managed to provide just the right combination of enthusiasm, encouragement, laughter, and sympathy. Our children, Alison and Mark, fueled my desire to pursue a career that enabled me to be home after school every day. Over fifteen years later, that move to freelance web design made this book possible. Both are exceptional writers, and occasionally a turn of phrase in one of their e-mail messages, social media posts, or conversations would inspire me to rework a sentence.

Amazingly and unfailingly, so many were kind enough to inquire about my progress with every conversation. My parents, Rosel and Irv, endured a seemingly endless series of lunch dates and phone calls where I rambled on at length about the process. Their support and enthusiasm have been strong from the moment I floated the concept of this book. They have been waiting many years to say "my daughter, the author" and now it has become a reality. It was at their kitchen table that the phrase "web diva wisdom" was first uttered.

Several friends and clients are published authors or have worked in the publishing industry. Their feedback, advice, and insights into the writing process were invaluable. They may not have realized it, but watching their successes provided inspiration, successful behaviors to model, and evidence that perseverance pays off.

So many of the important people in my life acted as informal sounding boards, patiently listening to the never-ending stories of trials, challenges, and occasional setbacks. They were not required to invest time in listening and providing support—but they did it anyway. Whether by phone or e-mail, over coffee, dinner, or frozen yogurt, or on train rides or car journeys where they had no means of escape, every one of them took the time to ask questions, listen, smile, and "uh-huh" appropriately at some point in the process. Somehow a guide to working with web designers managed to fit into mah jongg games, theater intermissions, gym sessions, nail appointments, and book club meetings. Thank you all for making me feel that this was appropriate discussion material at each occasion.

I appreciate the listening and feedback skills of so many, but especially want to recognize my sister Sharon, as well as my good friends Karen, Margaret, Doug, Jenn, Sue, Jessica, Esther, Bob, Carol, Paula, Rob, Scott, and Eddie.

And finally, I am grateful to my team at Createspace—from editing to design to production—for working with this novice to get through the maze that is the publishing process, and to provide much-needed counsel. Their attention helped make this material that much more readable and useful.

About the Author

Lisa Stambaugh has been a freelance web diva for over fifteen years, during which time she has designed and implemented more than five hundred websites. Previously she held individual contributor and management positions in engineering, quality, and information technology, spanning almost twenty years, at technology leaders as well as start-up endeavors.

She holds a BS in electrical engineering from the University of California, San Diego, and an MS in computer science from Stanford University. She lives in Fremont, California, with her husband Mike and a room full of computers. They have two adult children, Mark and Alison, and a menagerie of grandpets.

Made in the USA
Charleston, SC
03 June 2014